G.I.F.T.S.

G.I.F.T.S.

EMPOWER YOUR JOURNEY WITH FIVE KEYS OF TRANSFORMATION

Elaine Lombardi

MEL BOOKS

MEL BOOKS
2234 Via Puerta, Unit H
Laguna Woods, CA 92637

Copyright © 2024 by Elaine Lombardi

First Printing, 2024

All Rights Reserved. No part of this publication may be reproduced, distributed, or transmitted in any form or by any means, including photocopying, recording, or other electronic or mechanical methods without the prior written permission of the publisher, except in the case of brief quotation embodied in critical reviews and certain other noncommercial use permitted by copyright law. For permission requests contact the Author Elaine Lombardi.
Email: elaine@elainelombardi.com
Website:www.ElaineLombardi.com

ISBN 978-0-9861287-7-6
FIRST EDITION, AUGUST 2024

Library of Congress Cataloging-in-Publication Data
Lombardi, Elaine
G.I.F.T.S. :Empower Your Journey with Five Keys of Transformation / written by Elaine Lombardi

Summary: Insightful strategies for embarking on a healing journey to heal childhood wounds, and unlock a newfound sense of purpose, passion, joy, and fulfillment by using five keys of transformation that led to the formation of the G.I.F.T.S. method shared in this book.

Cover Design by Amina N. @design_erya

The content of this book is for general instructions only Each person's physical, emotional, and spiritual condition is unique The instructions in this book are not intended to replace or interrupt the reader's relationship with a physician or other professional. Please consult your doctor for matters pertaining to your specific health and wellness.

Lombardi, Elaine
G.I.F.T.S. Empower Your Journey with Five Keys of Transformation / Elaine Lombardi
ISBN-13: 978-0-9861287-7-6 (trade pbk: alk paper) 1. Purpose 2. Passion 3. Fulfillment
4 Transformation 5. Childhood Trauma 6. Well-Being I. Lombardi, Elaine II. Title

This book is dedicated to

My dear husband, Michael Lombardi

Honey, as I reflect on the journey of writing this book,
I am grateful for your unwavering love and support over
the five-plus decades we've shared together.

You have been my rock, standing by my side as
I confronted the demons of my past.
Your belief in me never wavered, even when
my confidence faltered. Your quiet strength and
devotion have been my guiding light.

This book is a testament to the depth of our partnership
and the beautiful life we've built together.
You are my best friend and the most
incredible father to our children.

Thank you for loving me unconditionally and for believing
in my dreams. I am forever grateful and blessed
to have you in my life as my husband and soulmate.

I love you with all my heart.

Contents

Dedication	v
A NOTE FOR YOU	ix
ROOTS Of INFLUENCE	1
1 Echoes of Childhood Memories	3
2 Stages of Childhood	13
3 Motivations, Values and Beliefs	19
4 The Power of Affirmations	33
5 The Art of Journaling	39
THE G.I.F.T.S. METHOD	49
6 Five Keys of Transformation	51
KEY OF GRATITUDE	59
7 The Powerful Gift of Appreciation	61
8 Cultivating a Gratitude Practice	71
KEY OF INTUITIVE INTENTION	87
9 The Gift of Being the Architect of Your Life	89
10 The Nature of the Ego and the Soul	105
11 Self-Sabotaging Behaviors	115
KEY OF FAMILY AND FRIENDS	123

12	The Gift of Family, Friends, and You	125
13	Personality Development	135
14	Self-Worth, Self-Confidence, and Self-Esteem	147
15	Strengthening Communication	159
16	Marriage and Family	175

KEY OF TREASURED WISDOM		183
17	The Key of Knowledge and Insight	185
18	Journey to Unlock Your Treasured Wisdom	191
19	Envision Your Best Day Ever	195

KEY OF SELF-LOVE & CARE		199
20	Nurturing the Gift of Self-Love & Care	201
21	Adopting a Rejuvenating Sleep Ritual	205
22	Healthy, Mindful Eating Habits	209
23	Exercise Made Easy	219
24	Personal Hygiene and Radiant Skin	225
25	Designing a Nurturing Self-Care Plan	235
26	Path to Purpose Passion, Joy, and Fulfillment	241
Conclusion		249

About The Author   251

A NOTE FOR YOU

Dear Reader,

As you begin your journey of self-discovery, empowerment, and transformation, I encourage you to acknowledge the profound influences that your past experiences have had on shaping the person you are today. Your upbringing, the relationships you form, and the lessons you learn all contribute to the fabric of your life.

If you've ever felt stuck in the rut of routine, longing for something more but unsure of where to start, this book is for you. If you've ever questioned your worth or doubted your abilities, this book is for you. If you've ever yearned for deeper connections, greater clarity, and a renewed sense of purpose, this book is for you.

Through heartfelt storytelling, practical insights, and actionable steps, this book guides you on a journey of self-discovery, empowerment, and transformation. As you immerse yourself in the pages ahead, I wholeheartedly invite you to explore the depths of your past, the possibilities of your present, and the limitless potential of your future, so that you can emerge with a newfound sense of clarity, confidence, and purpose.

This book is not only about finding answers. It's about asking yourself the right questions. It's about recognizing the profound impact your childhood experiences have on the way you navigate the world now, as an adult. It's about acknowledging any wounds you may have carried from your past into adulthood and finding the courage to heal from them. It's about embracing the power of choice and reclaiming control over your destiny. It's about embracing the journey of self-discovery with an open heart and a willingness to change, not who you are, but what no longer serves you. And finally, it's about reclaiming your power and stepping boldly into the life you are meant to live.

Imagine a future where you stand tall in the face of adversity, while guided by intentions fueled by your innate intuition, and unwavering determination. Picture yourself surrounded by heart-centered relationships that uplift and inspire you, propelling you forward on your journey with courage and grace.

As I sit here writing these words, I am reminded of how discovering the five golden keys that make up the G.I.F.T.S. method transformed my life. From this place of self-reflection and introspection, I am compelled to share with you the insights and wisdom I gathered throughout my journey.

The first key, Gratitude, unlocked the gift of appreciating the blessings in my life and cultivating a positive mindset. Through the daily practice of checking in with myself, releasing limiting beliefs, and focusing on the positives, I shifted my perspective by embracing the healing potential of positive thinking. This in turn radiates positivity and gratitude to those around me.

The second key, Intuitive Intention, unlocked the gift of aligning my actions with my inner wisdom and values. This empowered me to make mindful choices that honor my well-being and authenticity, allowing me to positively influence others by example.

The third key, nurturing relationships with Family and Friends, unlocked the gift of discovering the importance of connection and support in fostering emotional and spiritual growth. Meaningful connections with family and friends became essential pillars in my healing journey. Through these relationships, I learned the power of empathy and compassion that extends beyond myself.

The fourth key, Treasured Wisdom, unlocked the gift of seeking knowledge and insights that nourished my soul. I also uncovered a treasure trove of generational wisdom collected within myself, which I am blessed to share with others and contribute to the collective wisdom of humanity.

And the fifth key, Self-Love & Care, unlocked the gift of prioritizing self-care and embracing self-compassion. By putting my oxygen mask on first I cultivated a deep sense of worthiness and inner peace. That enabled me to show up more fully for others and contribute positively to my community and the world.

In embracing and embodying these principles, I have experienced profound growth and transformation that extends far beyond my own life. Today, I am dedicated to spreading the message of holistic wellness, encouraging you to unlock your inner wisdom and live authentically, while guided by timeless principles that benefit not only yourself but also the world.

This book isn't solely about my journey and the stories I share. It's about your journey and the narrative you're telling yourself. Our stories are a testament to the resilience of the human spirit and the infinite potential for growth within each of us. This book provides a roadmap for anyone who dreams of a purposeful, joyful, and fulfilling life. Please share this book with anyone who may benefit from it.

So, dear reader, are you ready to embark on your transformative journey with me? If so, let's begin.

All my best,
Elaine

ROOTS of INFLUENCE

"A tree's beauty lies in its branches,
but its strength lies in its roots."
– Matshona Dhliwayo

"It's the little moments in childhood that makes the biggest memories."
– Author Unknown

1

Echoes of Childhood Memories

As you begin your journey of self-discovery, empowerment, and transformation, I encourage you to acknowledge the profound influences that your past experiences have had on shaping the person you are today. Your upbringing, the relationships you form, and the lessons you learn all contribute to the fabric of your life.

Think back to your earliest memories. Do you recall the warmth of your parent's embrace, the laughter you shared with your siblings, and the safety of the familiar place you called home? Perhaps instances of conflict, loneliness, or fear more readily come to your mind. Memories from your upbringing lay the foundation for your self-perception and worldview in these crucial formative years.

Positive Environment

Growing up in a household brimming with love and support lays a sturdy foundation for your emotional and social development. In such an environment, kindness is not just a virtue; it is a way of life that is woven into your daily interactions. Encouragement becomes second nature as it flows freely like a gentle stream, nurturing your sense of self and fostering your growth. In this nurturing atmosphere, trust blossoms naturally.

The presence of your parents and caregivers who offer unconditional love and support creates a sense of safety where vulnerability is embraced rather than feared. You feel secure in expressing yourself authentically, knowing that your thoughts, feelings, and experiences will be met with understanding and validation.

By witnessing acts of kindness and generosity firsthand, you learn the value of caring for others allowing you to extend a helping hand to those in need. You develop a deep understanding of emotions through your interactions with family members and learn to navigate relationships with sensitivity and grace.

These positive childhood experiences instill a deep sense of worthiness and belonging. You grow up knowing that you are valued and cherished for who you are, unconditionally accepted, and celebrated in all your uniqueness. This sense of belonging provides a sturdy anchor as you navigate the challenges of adolescence and step into adulthood.

As an adult, you carry with you the gifts of trust, authenticity, empathy, and self-worth. Armed with these invaluable attributes, you are better equipped to develop meaningful connections, pursue your passions, and contribute positively to the world.

Negative Environment

In contrast, one of the primary consequences of growing up in an environment where conflict, instability, fear, or neglect are prevalent is the tendency to hide your true feelings. When you witness or experience conflict, instability, or neglect as a child, you may learn to mask your emotions to protect yourself from further harm.

This learned behavior can become a coping mechanism, as you internalize the belief that expressing yourself freely could lead to negative consequences, causing you to suppress your emotions or express them in destructive or distorted ways. Trusting others becomes a significant challenge for you. You tend to become guarded or suspicious of others' intentions. It's a trait that results from experiencing betrayal, neglect, or abuse, which can sometimes lead to you mistreating others.

Living in an environment where conflict, instability, or neglect is prevalent, can create a constant sense of fear and uncertainty. You may perceive the world as a dangerous and unpredictable place, always on guard for potential threats or harm that may occur. Your fear and uncertainty can manifest in various ways such as anxiety, phobias, or difficulty in sleeping. You may exhibit high-stress response behaviors such as; irritability, aggression, or withdrawal.

The impact of growing up in this conflict-riddled environment extends beyond individual experiences and could influence how you view the world, often leading to a negative mindset and difficulty navigating new experiences with confidence.

As you can see, your childhood experiences shape the beliefs you have about yourself, others, and the world. The patterns of behaviors you form throughout your childhood can persist well into your adulthood.

The Negativity Bias

While we all may experience moments of joy and security, we are also not immune to the inevitable trials and tribulations of growing up in a complex society. Even in the most loving households, there may be conflicts, setbacks, or moments of uncertainty that shape your worldview.

Despite this, the human brain has a natural tendency to pay more attention to negative stimuli than positive ones, a bias often referred to as "negativity bias." This negativity bias evolved as a survival mechanism helping you detect and respond to potential threats in your environment.

As a result, negative experiences may leave a more significant imprint on your memory and cognition, leading you to recall them more readily than positive experiences. Negative events often evoke strong emotions, which can make them more memorable such that they overshadow the positive experiences you have had. If negative experiences were repeatedly reinforced by emotional turmoil, they may become deeply ingrained in your memory, while positive experiences that were not consistently reinforced fade into the background.

Dwelling on negative experiences from your childhood serves as your coping mechanism for unresolved emotional issues or trauma. Revisiting these memories, although painful, may offer you a sense of validation or control over these past events, even if it perpetuates negative thought patterns or emotional distress.

Childhood Trauma

For a child who has faced a traumatic event during their formative years, looking back on childhood can be a complex and emotional journey. Memories of innocence may be intertwined with moments of fear, confusion, or pain. The impact of trauma can cast a long shadow over how you perceive your past.

Personal Story: *Reflecting on my Childhood*

I have long carried the weight of an incident that I believed stemmed from overhearing a single childhood conversation. This moment profoundly shaped my path, identity, and sense of belonging, permeating every aspect of my existence and leaving me feeling unloved and disconnected. However, as I've embarked on my healing journey, I've come to realize that I can stop giving it the power to dictate my life.

I remember vividly the day it all unfolded. I was sitting in the waiting room outside the principal's office and overheard the dialogue that would reshape my perception of self-worth and belonging. This was the third school my brother and I had been shuffled to, and the stakes could not have been higher.

"I'm worried about what holding my son back a grade in school will do to his self-esteem," my mother's voice trembled with concern.

The principal's response, though expected, still struck a nerve. My brother was considered too far behind to move forward and would need to repeat the fourth grade. What followed shook me to my core.

A resounding thud echoed through the office, indicating my mother's fierce determination.

"Then you must also hold Elaine back so they remain two years apart in grade levels," my mother insistently exclaimed.

Her words hung heavy in the air. There was no reason to hold me back. The principal explained that I excelled in all areas academically and I was ready for the third grade. She emphasized that since I was already 8 ½ years old, with a February birthday that would have me turn 9, I would be much older than the students in second grade. My mother's resolve was unwavering. And just like that, my fate was sealed. The hurt of being unjustly placed where I did not belong cut deep, leaving scars that would last a lifetime.

As I navigated through elementary school, I felt like an outsider, ashamed of being older than my peers. Desperate to blend in, I concealed my true self beneath layers of pretense, pretending to be shy to avoid standing out. Whenever age was mentioned, I deflected attention, often suppressing my intellect to fit in with my younger peers. I endured teasing remarks such as, "Cat got your tongue?" by keeping my thoughts and aspirations hidden. During a classmate's birthday party, I refrained from taking a goodie bag, feeling unworthy due to my older age.

I had difficulty making friends because I thought the differences in our ages made it impossible to truly connect. The long-term effects of my mother's decision to hold me back a year in school, without considering how it would affect me, extended beyond that specific moment. This disheartening childhood trauma influenced how I saw myself, my ability to relate to others, and how I navigated each new milestone year after year.

Reflecting on my childhod, I've come to understand that healing isn't about erasing painful memories but about acknowledging them and reclaiming the stories that define me. It's about finding light in the darkness, recognizing my resilience, and having the courage to restore my sense of self-worth.

When I look back, I see that my childhood was more than just the disheartening trauma I endured. It was a journey marked by strength, growth, and an unwavering spirit of determination. Each step forward in my healing journey has been shaped by the challenges I faced, showing me how my capacity for compassion, both for myself and others, has grown.

To those on a similar path, I encourage you to embrace the complexity of your childhood story, honor your emotions, and hold onto the glimmers of light that guide you toward healing.

The Myth of a Perfect Childhood

There is no such thing as a perfect childhood. Your upbringing is unique, and your childhood is shaped by a variety of factors including; your family dynamics, interactions at school, relationships with peers, exposure to media, societal norms, socioeconomic status, cultural background, and your own temperament.

It's natural to look back on your childhood and wish it had been ideal. Perhaps you were influenced by portrayals of the "perfect" childhood in TV shows, movies, books, and ads. A typical ideal may be a house with a backyard, loving and involved parents, family vacations, and a stable, happy life. This image can stick in your mind, making you yearn for similar perfect experiences. But the reality is that it is an unrealistic standard.

Every child faces their own set of difficulties and challenges while growing up. Maybe your parents argued or separated, perhaps money was tight, or maybe a family member faced an illness. Maybe your parents worked long hours and weren't always available, or you experienced other tough circumstances. Clutching onto the belief that you were deprived of a "perfect" upbringing or that your family and experiences were deeply flawed, can lead to resentment. When real life doesn't match the idealized scenes seen on screens or in glossy magazines, it's easy to feel like you missed out.

But here's the truth: every childhood is a mix of good and bad moments, joy and struggles, and happy times and hardships. This mix is normal and necessary. It's how we learn resilience and coping skills. An actual perfect childhood, devoid of problems, would be unnatural.

Instead of holding onto an unattainable idea of perfection, it's more worthwhile to cherish the positive memories of your childhood while recognizing that all families face challenges. Your childhood may not have been picture-perfect, but it was real and meaningful despite the imperfections. Letting go of the myth of perfection frees you from unrealistic expectations and allows you to embrace the richness of your own unique childhood experiences.

Revisiting Happy Memories

When embarking on healing from a difficult childhood, it is imperative to acknowledge that even amidst the hardships, there were likely moments that sparkled with joy, warmth, and positivity.

Trauma, abuse, neglect, and unstable environments can weigh heavily and cast long shadows. However, the remarkable human spirit still finds ways to create moments of brightness and comfort, even in the darkest of circumstances. It may have been as simple as the kindness of a special teacher, the freedom of losing yourself in a favorite hobby or game, or the uncomplicated laughter shared with childhood friends.

Whatever the cherished memories, reflecting on these happier times can be incredibly powerful for the healing process. Accessing those joyful recollections evokes feelings of contentment, comfort, and even nostalgia that your younger self once knew as moments of peace, safety, and acceptance.

In doing the crucial work of processing anguish and adverse experiences, it is easy to overlook or minimize the precious positive touchstones of your childhood. But, engaging with positive memories will help balance and nourish your soul. It reassures you that despite challenges, you still had important childhood experiences like playing, exploring, and finding contentment.

Reminiscing on these lighter moments prevents you from feeling stuck in deprivation or overwhelmed by the shadows of your past suffering. Your happy memories become a healing salve and a way to self-soothe yourself, bolster hope, and tap into the sacred wellsprings of resilience you innately possess.

Whether through conscious therapeutic exercises or spontaneous flashes of poignant nostalgia, connecting with the childlike joys that shaped your earliest self provides comfort, pleasure, and renewal. It gives you the permission you need to celebrate your survival while honoring the worries and wonderment of your inner child.

Personal Story: *Finding Solace Amidst Turmoil*

For me, revisiting one particular happy childhood memory serves as a form of stress relief. It helps ease feelings of anxiety and tension. I recall when my mother took my brother and me to our local library. While my brother occupied himself catching pollywogs in the pond just outside, my mother accompanied me into the library to borrow storybook albums to take home and listen to on my record player. I repeatedly borrowed the Disney classic 'Bambi.'

As I gazed at the pictures on each page, eagerly anticipating the beep signaling of when to turn to the next page, I became fully absorbed in the enchanting tale as the narrator read me the story about Bambi's adventures in the forest. Bambi's journey of resilience, from facing loss and hardship to triumph, deeply resonated with me.

I identified with Bambi's experiences of isolation and longing for connection, finding validation and empowerment through his growth and transformation. The story's emphasis on the serene beauty of nature as a source of healing mirrored my own yearning for moments of peace amidst family chaos. The whimsical sounds of the forest, the gentle rustling of leaves, and the chirping birds created a sense of tranquility that I found deeply comforting.

Bambi's friendships with Thumper and Flower highlighted my desire for companionship, connection, and understanding. Ultimately, Bambi's story provided me with a beacon of hope.

Little did I know that at that time, this childhood memory would unfold in real-time during a pivotal moment, marking the enlightened beginning of my healing journey. As I reflect on these memories, I am reminded of my capacity to find joy in life's simple pleasures, fostering resilience and well-being amidst life's trials.

Self Reflection Exercise

As you reflect on your own childhood memories, I invite you to pause and consider the following questions:

- What are some of the earliest recollections that stand out most vividly in your mind?

- Can you recall specific sensations, sights, or sounds that take you back to those formative years?

- How do these memories, whether joyful or challenging, continue to influence your perspectives and behaviors today?

Take a moment to journal about one or two of your most impactful childhood experiences. Describe the setting, the emotions you felt, and how that moment has shaped the person you are today. By connecting with your personal history in this way, you can begin to uncover the impact of your early life experiences. By taking the time to examine your childhood memories, both positive and negative, you empower yourself to gain a deeper understanding of the root beliefs, that drive your behaviors, and contribute to your sense of self.

"Healing your inner child will help you rewrite your past and find the joy that is your birthright."
— Louise Hay

2

Stages of Childhood

It's important to realize that the significance of your childhood is not confined to one specific period of time. Human development is a complex journey influenced by many factors that affect various stages. These factors include biological, psychological, social, and environmental elements, all of which shape your identity, behaviors, and experiences dynamically.

From infancy, where biological and early caregiver interactions lay the foundation to adolescence, where biological changes, social dynamics, and identity exploration become paramount. Each stage plays a crucial role in shaping your identity, beliefs, and behaviors.

Infancy

During infancy, primary influences stem from your biological makeup and early interactions with your parents and caregivers. Biological factors such as genetics, prenatal environment, nervous system, and brain development provide the foundation for physical, neurological, and cognitive growth. As a baby, quality of care, attachment patterns, and early social interactions all play a crucial role in shaping your emotional development and forming the basis for future relationships.

These primal impressions set the groundwork for either healthy self-esteem and attachment or struggle with abandonment.

Toddler and Early Childhood

As a toddler, you begin absorbing messages about your self-worth and your place in the world through your earliest interactions. Love and care from your parents and caregivers plant the initial feelings of being valued, understood, and safe. Otherwise you may feel neglected, burdensome and lacking a secure bond. In early childhood, you start internalizing beliefs about your basic traits, abilities, and autonomy that become solidified blueprints for navigating life.

Elementary School Years

As you move through your elementary school-age years, your social environment expands to include peers, educators, and other significant figures outside your family unit. During this time you learn societal norms, values, and behavioral expectations through observation, imitation, and direct instruction which shape your beliefs, traditions, and sense of identity.

A child lavished with patience, encouragement, and opportunities to explore will more easily cultivate independence, confidence, and a self-image of being capable. Conversely, overly critical, controlling, or neglectful parenting can breed beliefs that you are inept and unworthy of freedom and exploration. You will doubt your innate skills.

Your middle childhood represents a period of rapid cognitive, emotional, and social development. Educational experiences, peer relationships, and extracurricular activities become prominent influences on knowledge and skills.

Pre-Adolescence and Teenage Years

The interplay between biological changes, social dynamics, and individual identity exploration becomes particularly pronounced as you enter adolescence. Hormonal shifts, brain development, and physical maturation drive the onset of puberty and shape your emerging sense of self. Peer influence intensifies as you seek acceptance, validation, and belonging within peer groups, which can influence your behaviors.

It is during this time that you strive for autonomy and independence while still relying on parental guidance and support. Cultural influences, individual temperament, and social competency for navigating the wider world interact and affect your mental health and overall well-being.

Media influences also play a pivotal role in shaping your attitudes, beliefs, and aspirations regarding gender roles, body image, career choices, and social ideals. Throughout these developmental stages, your personality, resilience, and genetic predispositions interact with your environment. These affect your academic achievement, and interpersonal relationships, now becoming the foundation for who you are and how you navigate your growing changes.

As you transition into your teenage years, you become more self-conscious, which can amplify the impact of external influences during these years. Success or failure in developing autonomy, healthy relationships, sexuality, and identity depends greatly on the underlying self-beliefs you formed about yourself. If the roots are strong and stable, weathering your teenage years is smoother. However deep wounds of low self-worth, poor confidence, and insecurity make it harder to thrive during this time.

Personal Story: *Unexpected Changes*

One of the most confusing experiences I went through was unexpectedly getting my period, soon followed by rapid body changes. Because I had been held back a year in school, I was older than my classmates, and no one prepared me for what to expect as I entered puberty. All of this was part of the following year's curriculum, but I faced it alone and felt scared and overwhelmed.

Confronting the realities of my developing body ahead of my peers profoundly impacted my growing-up years. I hid my budding breasts and curves beneath oversized shirts, thinking my fuller shape made me look fat. Each year, the school nurse would weigh us, and I became acutely aware that my number was higher than my classmates. I told my mother I needed to go on a diet, and she played along by cooking me a plain, dry hamburger without the bun and plain steamed green beans. Yuck! My attempts at dieting led to frustration, body image issues, and distorted eating patterns that lingered throughout my adolescence and well into adulthood.

Being held back a year in school had far-reaching consequences beyond the classroom. It meant I faced the challenges of puberty without the support and information provided to my peers. This isolation and lack of preparation left lasting scars, shaping my self-image and eating habits for years to come.

Your Inner Child's Beliefs

You carry your inner child with you throughout your whole life. From the values instilled by your parents to the cultural norms and societal expectations that surround you, each influence plays a role in shaping your understanding of yourself, others, and the world.

The roots of your most deeply held beliefs form during your formative childhood years. The relationship between your experiences and the self-beliefs you carry with you into adulthood is complex. But at the core, the seeds that now bloom as your fundamental self-perceptions, both positive and negative, were planted during your childhood.

How you interact with others affects how you view yourself and whether you believe your talents to be praiseworthy or undesirable. The messages you absorb about how you see yourself, your value in the world, your strengths, your lovability, and your talents become powerfully internalized and leave an indelible mark on your psyche.

While you can reshape deep-seated self-beliefs over time, your childhood was a uniquely impactful time that took root within you. Cultivating self-awareness of these lingering influences takes compassion, insight, and a willingness to examine and rewrite the narratives that no longer serve you.

I faced traumatic challenges and experiences in my childhood. These left lasting imprints on my values and beliefs, which hindered my ability to embrace my true self. Through self-reflection and introspection, I uncovered valuable lessons that contribute to my personal growth and resilience on the stepping stones of life's challenges and triumphs.

My childhood experiences have fueled my curiosity. They have ignited a determination and desire in me to embark on the journey of getting to know myself on a very deep level to heal and live authentically.

As you embark on your own journey of self-discovery and empowerment, I encourage you to unpack your beliefs, challenge your assumptions, and rewrite the narratives that no longer serve you. By acknowledging the complexity of your childhood and embracing both the joyful and difficult moments, you can gain valuable insights that will empower you to grow, heal, and thrive.

Your past does not define you, but it has undoubtedly shaped you. I encourage you to harness your experiences, both the positive and the negative. Use them as a catalyst for transformation.

Moving forward, I'm excited to introduce you to strategies and helpful exercises to explore your values and underlying beliefs. I will help you understand your motivations, and show you tools and effective practices to address limiting beliefs that no longer serve you in order to shift your mindset using the power of affirmations.

"The child in you, like all children loves to laugh, to be around people who can laugh at themselves, and to feel safe"

– Wayne Dyer

3

Motivations, Values and Beliefs

Self-awareness is about taking an honest look inward to understand your thoughts, feelings, behaviors, and motivations at a deep level. It involves observing yourself with open curiosity, diving into the roots of where your habits and reactions come from, or deciding if they are still valid and working for you. It involves deciding if it is time to update your mindset to evolve along with your growing self-knowledge.

By exploring yourself through the lens of self-awareness, you unlock insights into what matters most. With this understanding, you can then ensure your daily actions line up with your authentic principles. For example, if you notice areas where you've compromised your values for convenience or outside pressures, you can realign them. Self-awareness allows you to refine the values that represent your true self while shedding inauthentic ones picked up along the way.

As you navigate life's ups and downs, your values and beliefs may naturally shift. But by regularly tuning into your inner compass through self-reflection, you ensure your outer reality matches your inner truth.

The journey of self-discovery can feel intimidating at first. You may worry about what you'll uncover by taking an honest look within. But ultimately, the revelations awaiting you are priceless gifts. Getting in touch with your authentic values and beliefs provides the clarity to stop drifting through life. Instead, you can start living with deeper intention and purpose. From this self-understanding flows the power to author your own life in alignment with values and updated beliefs that will allow you to create a life of truth, meaning, and fulfillment.

Self Reflection Exercise

To get started, first consider the activities, experiences, or causes that ignite a fire within you and make you feel the most alive and engaged. Take a moment to ask yourself:

- What brings me a deep sense of purpose and fulfillment?

- Am I motivated by a desire to help others? Create something meaningful? Live a life of adventure and exploration?

Through self-awareness, you can uncover and articulate the motivations that inspire you to take action. By aligning the choices you make with your deepest desires and aspirations it motivates you to pursue what truly matters to you. Motivation serves as the driving force behind your actions. When you understand yourself deeply and make decisions that resonate with your true self, you operate from a place of authority and authenticity.

Examining your thoughts, emotions, and behaviors with clarity and objectivity involves recognizing your strengths and weaknesses as well as understanding how your values and beliefs shape your perceptions and interactions. It requires honesty, courage, and a willingness to confront the often uncomfortable truths that lie deep within yourself.

Self Reflection Exercise

Take a moment right now to sit in quiet contemplation, allowing your mind to wander back to your earliest memories. Ask yourself:

- What emotions arise as I revisit moments from my past?

- Are there patterns or themes I notice about my thoughts and behaviors?

By turning inward and exploring these questions with curiosity and compassion, you will begin to uncover the intricacies of your thoughts, feelings, and behaviors. Shining a light on patterns you notice can reveal their origins and and help you determine how they continue to influence your life today.

Consider, for example, how your childhood experiences may have influenced your beliefs about love and relationships. Ask yourself:

- Was I taught to value communication and emotional intimacy, or was I surrounded by examples of dysfunction and conflict?

These early lessons can shape your expectations, your fears, and your ability to form meaningful connections as an adult. Perhaps you've noticed recurring tendencies in your relationships or behaviors that stem from past experiences. For example, you may find that you struggle with trust issues in your relationships. This may be a pattern that traces back to early experiences of betrayal or abandonment.

Think about the messages you received about success and worthiness. Ask yourself:

- Was I encouraged to pursue my passions and dreams, or was I made to feel inadequate or unworthy of love and acceptance?

These ingrained beliefs can either propel you forward or hold you back in your endeavors. If you tend to seek validation from others, this may be a pattern that stems from a childhood environment where your worth was tied to external approval. By acknowledging these patterns, you can take proactive steps to break free from these limiting beliefs and behaviors.

Cultivating a deeper understanding of what truly matters to you enables you to become more resilient in the face of adversity and bounce back from setbacks with grace and perseverance more easily. When you know yourself intimately, by truly understanding your strengths, weaknesses, and unique qualities, it instills a sense of self-assurance that transcends external validation.

I encourage you to allow yourself to be open and honest with yourself. Acknowledge your fears, insecurities, and imperfections without judgment. Treat yourself with kindness, compassion, and understanding, especially in moments of struggle and self-doubt. And please, above all, practice self-compassion by offering yourself the same care and empathy that you would extend to a dear friend facing challenges.

Decoding Your Values and Beliefs

- **Values** represent what you hold dear and aspire to / whereas **beliefs** represent your understanding and interpretation of reality.

- **Values** guide your choices and actions / whereas **beliefs** inform your perspectives

Values

Your values are deeply held core assumptions, convictions, or ideals that shape your thoughts, attitudes, and behaviors as being meaningful and important to you. They are what you prioritize in life. Your values guide your decisions and actions, serving as a compass for how you live your life. They reflect what you consider to be desirable, worthy, and significant.

Values can encompass a wide range of ideals, including personal integrity, honesty, compassion, freedom, family, achievement, and social justice to name a few. Values influence various aspects of relationships, career choices, ethical decisions, and priorities.

Beliefs

Realize that what you believe to be true can often exist without concrete evidence. Your beliefs can be about yourself, others, or the world. Beliefs are formed through your experiences, observations, and your interpretations of events. Beliefs can be positive or negative, factual, or subjective, or empowering or limiting. While your underlying beliefs and limiting beliefs are related, they are characterized by distinct differences.

Underlying Beliefs

Underlying beliefs are often deeply ingrained and operate at a subconscious level, influencing your thoughts, feelings, and behaviors. They form the basis of how you interpret and make sense of your experiences. Examples of underlying beliefs might include beliefs about your worthiness, competence, safety, or the nature of your relationships.

Limiting Beliefs

On the other hand, limiting beliefs are a specific subset of your underlying beliefs that constrain and restrict your potential, growth, and ability to achieve your goals. Unlike underlying beliefs, limiting beliefs are negative and self-defeating in nature, creating barriers to your personal development and fulfillment. They arise from past experiences, fear of failure, or societal conditioning. Limiting beliefs can manifest as thoughts such as "I'm not good enough," "I don't deserve success and happiness," or "I'll never be able to change."

Values and Belief System

Your values and belief system are not static. They evolve, can be flexible, and may change over time as you gain new perspectives based on new information you believe to be true. They can change from new experiences and as you face unique challenges. The values and beliefs you hold dear in your childhood can shift and transform as you mature and develop a deeper understanding of yourself and the world around you. So, it's important to recognize that your values and beliefs are not set in stone. Rather, they are fluid and dynamic, shaped by the cumulative experiences that make up your life's journey.

Your values and beliefs serve as guiding lights. Reflecting on the origins of your values and beliefs can shed light on why you hold certain convictions dear. Understanding that values and beliefs can primarily be inherited from your upbringing and cultural environment, or from your life experiences and personal growth, will help you realize the complexity and diversity of your value system. Exploring the roots of your values and beliefs can help you discern which ones truly align with your authentic self, and which may have been shaped by external influences and societal conditioning.

This self-exploration allows you to consciously choose which values and beliefs to continuosly uphold and which ones may need to be re-evaluated or released so that you can live in greater alignment with your true nature. Furthermore, recognizing the fluidity of your values and beliefs empowers you to adapt and grow as you navigate the ever-changing landscape of your life.

When you cling rigidly to outdated beliefs, they can limit your ability to embrace new possibilities and opportunities for personal evolution. By remaining open and receptive to the evolution of your values and beliefs, you can cultivate the flexibility to respond to life's challenges with wisdom, empathy, and an expanding perspective.

I encourage you to explore the values and beliefs that are guiding your life decisions with honesty and self-compassion. Acknowledging which beliefs are empowering and which may be holding you back can shed light on the powerful forces that influence your thoughts, feelings, and actions.

Remember, your values and beliefs are not fixed. They evolve and transform as you grow and expand your self-awareness. By consciously choosing to uphold the values and beliefs that truly resonate with your authentic self, you empower yourself to live with greater purpose, fulfillment, and alignment with your deepest desires. Your journey of self-discovery is an ongoing process, but it's one that is immensely rewarding, as it allows you to claim ownership of your life and chart a course that is uniquely yours.

Addressing Limiting Beliefs

Addressing your limiting beliefs is a crucial step for your personal development. Limiting beliefs consist of the thought patterns and beliefs that hold you back from reaching your full potential. These beliefs are like invisible chains deeply rooted in your psyche. Many of your beliefs were formed during your childhood interactions with your parents, caregivers, peers, and authority figures.

For example, if as a child you constantly heard statements like "You'll never amount to anything" or "Money is the root of all evil," you may have internalized and held on to believing "I'm not qualified for that job", "Success is only for lucky people", "I'll never be wealthy", "Money is evil" to justify not taking action when faced with an opportunity to improve your financial situation.

Despite their restrictive nature, limiting beliefs often persist because they serve specific psychological functions that can feel comforting or protective in the short term. Understanding why you hold on to your limiting beliefs can shed light on their persistence and the challenges involved in letting them go.

Limiting beliefs provides a sense of safety by keeping you within your comfort zone. uncertainty and potential risks associated with stepping outside these boundaries. For example, believing "I'm not capable of leadership" might prevent you from pursuing a leadership role to avoid the challenges and responsibilities that come with being a leader. Likewise, believing "I'm not good at public speaking" prevents you from confronting the discomfort of failure or rejection associated with public speaking engagements.

Beliefs such as "I'll never succeed" or "I'm not worthy of love" can also serve as protective shields. By adopting these negative outlooks, you may believe you are sparing yourself from disappointment or hurt, but this form of self-preservation comes at the cost of missed opportunities and personal growth.

Past failures or traumas can also deeply impact your self-perception and beliefs about your capabilities. If you experienced a setback in your business you might adopt a belief that "I'm not cut out for entrepreneurship", which can deter you from pursuing future endeavors and new opportunities. Repetitive self-talk reinforces your limiting beliefs when you continuously tell yourself "I'm not good enough" or "I always mess things up." They only serve to solidify these beliefs in your subconscious, which in turn affects your confidence and willingness to take risks.

The impact of negative beliefs you have about your self-worth and confidence cannot be overstated. Over time, negative and limiting beliefs can erode your sense of self-esteem, creating self-fulfilling prophecies where your actions align with your limiting beliefs. For instance, believing "I'm unlovable" may lead you to sabotage your relationships or avoid intimacy altogether, reinforcing the initial belief that "I'm unlovable."

Moving beyond these limiting beliefs requires a conscious effort to challenge and reframe them. This involves questioning the validity of your beliefs, seeking counter-evidence that contradicts and challenges them, and engaging in positive self-talk and affirmations. By gradually confronting your fears and doubts, and taking small steps towards embracing new possibilities, you can begin to reshape your mindset and expand your sense of what is achievable.

While limiting beliefs may have served as a protective shield, at some point in your life, they ultimately hinder your personal growth and will continue to hold you back from realizing your true potential if you do not challenge and replace them with more positive and empowering beliefs. Understanding the origins of your negative thoughts and limiting beliefs, and actively cultivating a mindset that empowers you to break free from these constraints, enhances your self-worth and confidence to pursue a life of fulfillment and achievement.

Recognizing that beliefs are not permanent truths, but perceptions that can be reshaped through introspection and intentional action is key to overcoming these barriers. You are capable of embracing a more expansive and empowering self and worldview. Overcoming your limiting beliefs takes time and effort. So, be kind and compassionate with yourself throughout the process. Allow yourself to make mistakes and learn from them. Practice self-compassion and forgiveness, rather than beating yourself up for your past actions or failures.

Steps to Overcoming Limiting Beliefs

Recognizing that limiting beliefs can manifest in various ways, such as fear of failure, rejection, or change, is essential to overcoming them. Limiting beliefs permeate various aspects of your life and can significantly impact your self-perception, behavior, and overall well-being.

They often originate from early experiences, societal influences, and internalized messages that shape your belief system. Overcoming these limiting beliefs is crucial for personal growth and success. We all tend to seek out and remember information that confirms our existing beliefs because it serves to reinforce the validity of what we believe to be true. Our minds filter out evidence that contradicts our beliefs while amplifying evidence that supports what we believe to be true.

Limiting beliefs often have emotional associations. For instance, a belief like "I'm not worthy" may be tied to feelings of shame or inadequacy. By recognizing the sources of these beliefs and actively challenging them through introspection, seeking alternative perspectives, and embracing growth-oriented mindset shifts, you can begin to dismantle their grip on your life and cultivate empowering beliefs that align with your true potential and aspirations.

STEP ONE: *Identify Your Limiting Beliefs*

The first step in overcoming limiting beliefs is to identify them. Reflect on your past experiences and identify any negative thought patterns that hold you back. Limiting beliefs originate from various sources and can manifest in different areas of life, affecting your beliefs about yourself, relationships, career, health, and more. These beliefs often become ingrained in your belief system through repeated exposure to specific experiences, messages, or societal influences. Here's a deeper exploration of where some limiting beliefs come from across various areas of life:

> **Academic Performance**: A student who receives consistently low grades might develop a belief like "I'm not smart enough."
>
> **Artistic Talent**: Someone who is told early on that they lack artistic skills might adopt the belief, "I'm not creative."
>
> **Physical Abilities**: A person who struggles with sports may develop a belief such as "I'm not athletic."
>
> **Romantic Relationships**: Someone who has experienced heartbreak might adopt beliefs like "I'm unlovable" or "Love always leads to pain."
>
> **Friendships**: Individuals who have been betrayed or rejected by friends may develop beliefs such as "I can't trust anyone" or "I'm not good at making friends."
>
> **Career Limitations**: Beliefs like "I'm not qualified for that job"

or "Success is only for lucky people" can arise from societal expectations or past experiences of rejection.

Financial Beliefs: Growing up in a household where money was constantly scarce might lead to beliefs like "I'll never be wealthy" or "Money is evil."

Body Image: Exposure to unrealistic body standards in media can contribute to beliefs like "I'm not attractive" or "I'll never be fit."

Health Challenges: Someone dealing with chronic illness might develop beliefs such as "I'm always going to be sick" or "I can't overcome this health issue."

Gender Roles: Beliefs about what men and women can or cannot do based on societal norms, such as "Women aren't good at math" or "Men shouldn't show emotions."

Racial or Ethnic Stereotypes: Individuals may internalize limiting beliefs related to their race or ethnicity, such as "I'll always face discrimination" or "I can't achieve success in this country."

STEP TWO: *Challenge Your Limiting Beliefs*

Once identified, challenge them logically and rationally. Ask yourself:

- Is this belief based on fact or is it based on fear?

Challenge fact vs. fiction

It is important to separate fact from fiction and critically evaluate your beliefs. To distinguish between fact and fear objectively evaluate the evidence that supports and contradicts the limiting belief. Ask yourself:

- What specific experiences or observations led to this belief?

- Is there concrete evidence to support this belief?

- Are there instances where this belief has been disproven or challenged?

Challenge the driving force

Understand the emotional component driving this belief. Ask yourself:

- What emotions (fear of failure, rejection, inadequacy) are associated with this belief?

- How does this belief protect or validate these fears or insecurities?

Challenge the outcome

- Observe yourself and others objectively and assess the outcome.

- Identify instances where you have succeeded or performed well.

- Look for examples of others who have achieved success in a similar situation.

Optional: Consider asking for feedback from a trusted family member or friend who can offer you alternative perspectives. Continue to challenge your limiting beliefs by stepping out of your comfort zone and seeking new experiences. Take on new challenges and take risks that push you beyond your comfort zone. By pushing yourself beyond what you believe is possible, you can prove to yourself that your limiting beliefs are unfounded.

STEP THREE: *Replace Your Limiting Beliefs*

Once you have identified and challenged your limiting beliefs, replace them with positive and empowering beliefs. Instead of focusing on what could go wrong, focus on what is possible. Replace negative thoughts with positive statements using affirmations. Repeatedly saying thoughtful positive affirmations is a powerful technique used to replace limiting beliefs by reinforcing positive new beliefs.

Here's a list of affirmations specifically designed to replace the ingrained beliefs you may have adopted from childhood with positive, more empowering ones.

1. I release all limiting beliefs from my childhood and embrace my true potential.
2. I am worthy of love, success, and happiness, regardless of my past experiences.
3. I let go of any belief that I am not enough, and I fully accept myself as I am.
4. I am capable of achieving my dreams and creating the life I desire.
5. I choose to see challenges as opportunities for growth and learning.
6. I release the need to seek approval from others and trust in my own worth.
7. I am deserving of abundance in all areas of my life.
8. I believe in my abilities and have the confidence to pursue my passions.
9. I release any fear of failure and embrace the journey of self-discovery.
10. I am free to create new, empowering beliefs that align with my highest potential.

Most importantly, be kind to yourself. Recognize that you are worthy of love, success, and happiness.

BONUS: The following five additional affirmations specifically focus on fostering self compassion, empowerment, and healing to address more deep-seated childhood wounds. These affirmations help to foster a more positive and compassionate inner dialogue.

1. I am deserving of happiness, joy, and peace in my life.
2. I am capable of creating healthy and loving relationships.
3. I am enough just as I am, and I deserve to live a life of purpose and fulfillment.
4. I am worthy of seeking help and support when I need it.
5. I choose to release the pain of the past and embrace a future filled with healing and growth.

4

The Power of Affirmations

Using affirmations to reprogram your thoughts and deeply rooted beliefs reshapes your perception of yourself and your abilities. Affirmations work by intentionally introducing positive and supportive statements. Consistently repeating affirmations that affirm your desired thoughts, beliefs, and outcomes helps to embed them into your subconscious.

Studies have shown that affirmations have the potential to rewire and create new neural pathways, which are the connections between the neurons in your brain. These pathways play a significant role in releasing chemicals called neurotransmitters in your brain, such as serotonin and dopamine. These neurotransmitters are responsible for regulating your mood, motivations, and cognitive function. They shape your thoughts, emotions, and behaviors.

When you repeat an affirmation to yourself, your mind begins to process the repetitive messages as a pattern and starts to reinforce it. By consciously choosing to repeat positive statements, you train your brain to filter out negative thoughts and focus on more positive ones. Over time, these pathways become stronger and internalized. Repeating these positive thoughts can help break the cycle of negativity and improve your overall outlook on life.

Affirmations have the power to shift your mindset and empower you to take control of your thoughts and actions. When you repeat affirmations like "I am capable", "I deserve success", or "I am worthy of love" you begin to believe them. That can have a profound effect on your self-confidence and your self-esteem.

Using Visualization with Affirmations

Affirmations combined with visualization can synergize to amplify personal growth and manifestation. Affirmations can empower your beliefs and attitudes. But when paired with vivid mental imagery through visualization your affirmations become more potent.

This powerful combination not only boosts confidence, it also sharpens your focus and determination.

By consistently practicing affirmations with visualization, you overcome obstacles by reimagining the outcome which accelerates your transformation.

STEP ONE: *Mindful Selection of Affirmations*

Choosing affirmations that align with your personal goals and values is the first crucial step. Being super mindful about your selection ensures that the statements you say to yourself resonate on a deep, personal level, to create a strong emotional connection. Your affirmations need to be framed in the present tense and should emphasize positivity. For example, instead of saying, "I am not stressed," say, "I am calm and composed in all situations."

Here's a list of 25 affirmations covering various aspects of life. Choose the ones that resonate with you the most. Do not underestimate the power of simply starting with one to focus on allowing yourself the time to believe it down in your soul.

1. I am worthy of love and kindness.
2. I radiate confidence, self-respect, and inner harmony.

3. Every day, I am becoming a better version of myself.
4. I attract positive energy and opportunities into my life.
5. I am in control of my thoughts, and I choose positivity.
6. I am resilient, and I can overcome any challenges that come my way.
7. My potential is limitless, and I am capable of achieving my goals.
8. I am grateful for the abundance in my life.
9. I trust the process of life and let go of any resistance.
10. I am surrounded by supportive and uplifting people.
11. I am a magnet for success, and I attract success into my life effortlessly.
12. My mind is clear, focused, and full of creative ideas.
13. I am at peace with my past, present, and future.
14. I am deserving of all the good things that life has to offer.
15. I am a source of love and compassion.
16. I choose to let go of worry and embrace a sense of calm.
17. I am capable, strong, and resilient in the face of uncertainty.
18. I release all negative thoughts and embrace positivity.
19. I am in charge of my life, and I create my own happiness.
20. I trust in my ability to make the right decisions.
21. I am open to new experiences and opportunities for growth.
22. My body is healthy, and my mind is brilliant.
23. I am worthy of success in all areas of my life.
24. I am a beacon of light, and my positive energy inspires others.
25. I am constantly evolving and growing into the best version of myself.

STEP TWO: *Repetition and Visualization*

Repetition is key to embedding affirmations into your subconscious mind and initiating neuro changes. Consistent daily practice reinforces the positive messages, gradually replacing old thought patterns with your new desired affirmative thoughts. Visualization further enhances the effectiveness of your affirmations by engaging your brain in creating vivid mental images associated with the positive statements you say. This helps in reinforcing the emotional and sensory aspects of your desired outcome. Here are a few examples:

Affirmation: "I am worthy of love and kindness."
Visualization: Imagine yourself surrounded by a warm, golden light, symbolizing love and kindness. Feel this light enveloping you, starting from the top of your head and flowing down to your toes. Visualize yourself basking in this loving energy, feeling worthy, cherished, and deeply loved. See yourself embracing this feeling of worthiness and kindness, allowing it to fill every part of your being.

Affirmation: "I am capable, strong, and resilient in the face of uncertainty."
Visualization: Picture yourself standing tall and confident amidst a stormy sea. The waves crash around you, representing life's uncertainties and challenges. Despite the turbulence, visualize yourself rooted firmly to the ground, your stance unwavering. Feel a sense of inner strength and resilience radiating from within you, empowering you to weather any storm that comes your way. See yourself emerging from the turmoil stronger, more resilient, and ready to face whatever lies ahead.

Affirmation: "I am open to new experiences and opportunities for growth."
Visualization: Envision yourself standing in a lush, vibrant meadow. As you step forward, feel a sense of excitement and anticipation coursing through you. Each step you take represents openness to new experiences and opportunities for growth. Visualize yourself exploring, discovering hidden treasures, and embracing the unknown with curiosity and enthusiasm. See yourself expanding your horizons, embracing new challenges,

and growing in wisdom and understanding with each new experience.

STEP THREE: *Integration*

Incorporating affirmations into your daily routines ensures regular exposure and integration into your mindset. Methods such as reciting affirmations during meditation, saying them to yourself in the mirror during your morning routine, and doing a visualization right before bedtime can be very effective. Writing down your affirmations and posting them in prominent locations, such as on your bathroom mirror, a sticky note on your desk at work, and beside a kitchen cabinet you open daily, all serve as constant reminders.

The integration of affirmations into your daily activities strengthens the connection between the positive statements you say and your routine actions, to further facilitate the formation of new neural pathways in your brain. By replacing self-doubt with self-assurance and fear with courage, over time, you'll witness the transformative power of your thoughts as they shape your reality and pave the way for a brighter, more fulfilling future.

Your Thoughts Shape Your Reality

Your thoughts are powerful, so choose them wisely. They have the power to shape your reality and create the life you desire. Your thoughts are the bridge that connects your motivations to your reality. The way you think about yourself, your capabilities, and the world around you, has a profound impact on the experiences you create and the life you lead. Let's explore how the thoughts you think shape reality,

Have you ever noticed how when you wake up feeling positive and optimistic, the day ahead seems full of promise and opportunity? Your mind is clear, your energy levels are high, and you tackle challenges with confidence.

On the flip side when negative thoughts creep in, they cast a shadow over everything, draining your motivation and clouding your judgment. Think about a time when you were consumed by worry or self-doubt. Maybe you convinced yourself that you weren't good enough, or that failure was inevitable. How did your negative thoughts affect your behavior? Did these negative thoughts make you hesitate to take risks or hold you back from pursuing your goals?

Each thought, whether positive or negative, takes root and begins to grow. It shapes the perception of yourself and the world around you. When you dwell on negativity, you attract more of it into your life. Every time you entertain a negative thought, you give it power over you. This negativity seeps into your subconscious. It's like a self-fulfilling prophecy, where your beliefs shape your experiences. But the good news is that you can change your thoughts and in turn change your life.

When you choose positive thoughts of optimism, courage, and abundance, you nurture possibility. Your mind then becomes a garden teeming with potential, where every thought has the power to bloom. By consciously directing your thoughts toward what you desire, you can cultivate a mindset of empowerment.

Your thoughts are silent forces that influence your emotions, motivational actions, and ultimately your destiny. Pay attention to the thoughts that arise within you. Consciously choose to redirect them towards a more positive direction. Instead of dwelling on what's wrong, focus on appreciating what's right. Empower your thoughts to pave the way for a life filled with purpose, meaning, and joy.

Embarking on any journey involves navigating the vast seas of your thoughts, emotions, and experiences in a nonjudgemental space. Journaling is a great tool and a timeless practice that can serve as a trusty compass, guiding you through the depths of the thoughts within your inner world.

Journaling sets you free to express your fears, doubts, and insecurities without fear of being criticized or judged. This, in turn, helps you develop greater self-compassion and acceptance of who you are.

5

The Art of Journaling

As you begin your journey of self-discovery, empowerment, and transformation, I encourage you to acknowledge the profound influences that your past experiences have had on shaping the person you are today. Your upbringing, the relationships you form, and the lessons you learn all contribute to the fabric of your life.

Journaling is a powerful practice that involves using writing as a tool for personal growth, self-reflection, and self-improvement. Through journaling, you can explore your thoughts, emotions, beliefs, and experiences in a structured and intentional way. Whether you're setting goals, identifying areas for growth, or reflecting on lessons learned, journaling provides a safe and supportive space for deepening self-awareness and cultivating positive change.

By regularly engaging in self-development journaling, you can gain insights into yourself, clarify your values and priorities, track your progress, and take meaningful steps towards becoming the best version of yourself. Let's delve into various journaling techniques and tools that can help you make the most of your meaningful writing experience.

A technique called Morning Pages, in Julia Cameron's book "The Artist's Way" suggests that you start the day by writing three pages in a journal first thing in the morning.

Morning Pages

The idea is that "Morning Pages" prove, clarify, comfort, prioritize, and synchronize your day. Julia suggests not to overthink it. Just write three pages of anything that comes to mind on paper and then three more tomorrow to get into the habit of incorporating self-expression into your day. If you find yourself struggling with writer's block or feel stuck, she suggests keeping your pen on the paper to doodle until something comes to mind.

Doodling

I think doodling is a wonderfully expressive and therapeutic way to unleash your creativity and communicate your thoughts and feelings. Doodling is a form of spontaneous drawing that often occurs absent-mindedly, but, it can also be a deliberate, intentional practice.

Doodling serves as a visual language through which you can express yourself in a way that words alone cannot. It allows you to tap into your intuition, imagination, and creativity. It providers an outlet for self-expression and exploration. Whether you're feeling stressed, anxious, or simply bored, doodling offers a means of relaxation and escape, transporting you to a state of flow where time seems to stand still.

The beauty of doodling lies in its simplicity and accessibility. You don't need fancy art supplies or years of training to doodle. All you need is a pencil and a piece of paper. There are no rules or expectations when it comes to doodling. You're free to just let your imagination run wild and see where it takes you.

Doodling can take many forms, from abstract shapes and patterns to whimsical characters and scenes. Some people use doodling as a form of meditation, allowing their thoughts to flow freely as they draw. Others use it as a way to brainstorm ideas and visually map out concepts and connections.

One of the most wonderful aspects of doodling is its ability to promote mindfulness and presence. When you're immersed in the act of doodling, you're fully engaged in the present moment, allowing your mind to quiet down and your stress to melt away. It's a form of active meditation that can bring a sense of calm and clarity to your mind.

When doodling, pay attention to the shapes and symbols that emerge on the page. Consider using colored pencils to add color to your doodles. Notice how certain patterns repeat themselves or how your mood influences the direction of your doodles. You may uncover hidden insights about yourself and gain a deeper understanding of your emotions and experiences.

Choosing Your Journal

There's a wide variety of journals available on the market that cater to different preferences, needs, and purposes. Choosing the right journal is a personal decision that depends on your intended use. Here are some factors to consider when selecting a journal:

Purpose

Determine the primary purpose of your journaling practice. Are you looking to document your thoughts and experiences, cultivate gratitude, set goals, track habits, or explore your creativity? Clarifying your purpose will help you choose a journal that aligns with your goals and intentions.

Paper Quality

Pay attention to the paper quality of the journal, especially if you plan to write or draw with different types of pens or markers. Look for journals with thick, high-quality paper that won't show bleed marks on the other side.

Size

Decide on the size of the journal based on your preferences and intended use. Do you prefer a larger journal with ample space for writing and drawing, or a smaller and more portable journal that you can easily carry with you? Consider where you'll be journaling most often. Choose a size that fits your lifestyle.

Format

Consider the format of the journal that best suits your preferences and needs. Do you prefer a traditional bound journal with lined or blank pages, a spiral-bound notebook for easy flipping, or a compact journal that you can bring on the go? Think about how you plan to use the journal and choose a format that feels comfortable and convenient for you.

Guidance

Determine whether you prefer a journal with guided prompts, exercises, or themes to inspire your writing. Otherwise you might prefer a blank journal that allows complete creative freedom. Guided journals can be helpful for beginners or those seeking structure, while blank journals offer more flexibility for self-expression.

Journaling Prompts

There are several resources available online that offer journaling prompts and templates to help kick-start your practice. My book titled, **"Little Lessons, Big Life Journal"** is a keepsake journal available in hard cover or soft cover. This journal contains a collection of inspirational quotes and writing prompts that inspire you to explore your thoughts and journal your feelings. Included are diary pages, as well as areas to add photos.

Aesthetic

Consider the aesthetic appeal of the journal, including its cover design, color scheme, and overall look and feel. Choose a journal that resonates with your personal style and preferences, like whether you prefer a sleek and minimalist design, a vibrant and colorful pattern, or a classic and timeless look.

Additional Features

Look for any additional features or accessories that may enhance your journaling experience such as built-in bookmarks, elastic closures, pen loops, or pockets for storing mementos. These extra features can add convenience and functionality to your journal.

Price

Set a budget for your journal purchase and explore options within your price range. While there are journals available at various price points, remember that the value of a journal lies not only in its cost but also in one that feels comfortable, inspiring, and conducive to your journaling practice.

Writing Guide

Starting to write can sometimes feel daunting, but it doesn't have to be! Here are some simple steps to help you get started:

STEP ONE: *Set the Mood*

Find a comfortable and quiet space where you feel relaxed and inspired. Whether it's a cozy corner of your home, a peaceful park bench, or a bustling café, choose a location that fosters creativity and focus.

STEP TWO: *Clear Your Mind*

Take a few moments to clear your mind and center yourself. Practice deep breathing, meditation, or a short mindfulness exercise to quiet any distractions and prepare your mind for writing.

STEP THREE: Choose Your Topic

Decide what you want to write about. It could be a personal experience, a fictional story, or even a list of goals or ideas. Choose a topic that interests you and sparks your curiosity.

STEP FOUR: Set a Goal

Set a specific goal or intention for your writing session. It could be to write for a certain amount of time, reach a particular word count, or simply explore a topic in depth. Having a clear goal in mind will help keep you focused and motivated.

STEP FIVE: Start Writing

Let your thoughts flow freely onto the page without judgment or editing. If you're feeling stuck, try using writing prompts or doodling until something comes to mind that you feel compelled to write about.

Writing Topics to Explore

Journal writing serves as a profound companion on the path of healing and transformation as it offers a safe space for you to explore your inner landscapes and navigate the complexities of your emotions. Embarking on a healing and transformational journey often involves confronting past wounds, understanding current challenges, and envisioning a future filled with growth and resilience.

Through the art and act of journaling, you embark on a transformative process of self-discovery and self-expression. This intentional practice invites you to reflect on your experiences, process your feelings, and gain insights that lead to healing and personal growth. Whether it's healing from trauma, navigating life transitions, or seeking inner peace, journal writing becomes a therapeutic tool that empowers you to reclaim your narratives and cultivate greater self-awareness and understanding. Let's explore some topics you may wish to focus some of your writing time.

Gratitude Journaling

Gratitude journaling is a simple yet powerful practice that involves regularly writing down things you're thankful for. It's a way to cultivate a positive mindset. Setting aside a few minutes each day to reflect on the things you're grateful for, whether big or small, can range from the people in your life to the simple pleasures you enjoy. You could write about the moments of joy, acts of kindness you've received, accomplishments you're proud of, or even the challenges that have helped you grow. The key to gratitude journaling is to focus on what's positive and meaningful in your life, no matter how small or seemingly insignificant.

As you write you may notice shifts in your perspective and mindset. You may find yourself more attuned to the blessings in your life, more resilient in the face of challenges, and more present and appreciative of each moment. Over time, gratitude journaling can become a powerful tool for fostering happiness. Even on days when you're feeling down or uninspired, taking a few moments to focus on gratitude can make a world of difference in shifting your perspective and lifting your spirits.

Relationship Journaling

Relationship journaling is valuable as it focuses on exploring and nurturing your connections with others. Whether it's romantic relationships, friendships, family dynamics, or professional interactions, relationship journaling is an opportunity for you to reflect on the dynamics, challenges, and joys within your relationships.

Through relationship journaling, you can express your thoughts and feelings about your interactions with others, identify patterns or areas for improvement, and celebrate moments of connection and growth. Relationship journaling can assist you in exploring effective communication strategies.

Use your writing to express your feelings, reflect on conflicts, and navigate boundaries with empathy and understanding. By regularly engaging in relationship journaling, you can deepen your connections, strengthen your relationships, and foster greater intimacy and trust with the important people in your life.

Storytelling Journaling

Storytelling journaling is like crafting the narrative of your dreams, where you become the author of your life story. It's about envisioning the life you want to live by exploring different possibilities, and expressing your deepest desires and aspirations through storytelling.

In your journal, you can create characters who embody the qualities you admire, imagine settings that inspire you, and plot adventures that ignite your imagination. By engaging in storytelling journaling, you're not just writing stories, you're dreaming, manifesting, and shaping the narrative one page at a time.

Expressive Writing Styles

The art of journaling lies in its versatility, and just about any topic can become a vessel for self-expression. By adding some stylized writing techniques your journal becomes a playground where you can freely play and express yourself using various styles to suit different moods and purposes. Using several different styles as you write adds more depth to expressive writing.

Reflective Writing

Reflective writing is like having a conversation with your inner self. Use it to explore your thoughts, feelings, and experiences in a meaningful way. Take a moment to pause, breathe, and reflect on your day, relationships, or personal growth journey. Write journal entries that delve into your hopes, fears, joys, and struggles, allowing yourself to be vulnerable and honest on the page.

Creative Writing

Let your imagination run wild with creative writing. Use this style to unleash your creativity, play with language, and explore new worlds. Write poetry that captures the beauty of nature, short stories that transport you to far-off lands, or even snippets of dialogue between fictional characters. The sky's the limit when it comes to creative writing in your journal!

Descriptive Writing

This style is all about painting a vivid picture with your words. You can use descriptive writing to capture the sights, sounds, smells, and emotions of a moment. Imagine you're an artist with words, one who is creating a masterpiece on the page.

Narrative Writing

Narrative writing is similar to storytelling journaling but this style is more about recounting experiences, adventures, and memories that already happened. Examples would be to write about a memorable trip you took, a funny encounter you had, or a challenging situation you overcame.

Expository Writing

When you want to dive deep into a topic or explore your thoughts in a structured way, expository writing is your go-to style. Use it to break down complex ideas or analyze your beliefs.

Persuasive Writing

Sometimes, you might find yourself trying to convince yourself of something or motivate yourself to take action. That's where persuasive writing comes in handy. Use this style to make a case for your goals, aspirations, or self-improvement plans. Write persuasive journal entries that inspire you to chase your dreams, overcome obstacles, and become the best version of yourself.

Argumentative Writing

You don't always have to agree with yourself. Argumentative writing allows you to explore different perspectives and challenge your own beliefs. Use this style to engage in a thoughtful debate with yourself by weighing the pros and cons of a decision or exploring conflicting emotions. You might write journal entries debating whether to take a new job, questioning your values, or wrestling with a moral dilemma.

All of these different journaling topics and writing styles, as well as simply letting your mind wander by doodling, can have profound benefits for your mental, emotional, and spiritual well-being. I encourage you to use journaling throughout your journey.

THE G.I.F.T.S. METHOD

KEY OF
GRATITUDE

KEY OF
INTUITIVE INTENTION

KEY OF
FAMILY AND FRIENDS

KEY OF
TREASURED WISDOM

KEY OF
SELF-LOVE & CARE

6

Five Keys of Transformation

At the heart of the G.I.F.T.S. method are five golden keys, each representing an essential aspect of living a fulfilling and joyous life. The term **G.I.F.T.S.** serves as an acronym for **G**ratitude, intuitive **I**ntention, your relationships with **F**amily and friends, your **T**reasured wisdom, and **S**elf-love & Care. These five keys work together to unlock a realm of gifts and new possibilities that guide you toward a deeper sense of wholeness and balanced harmony within yourself and the world.

Periodically, throughout my life, I ventured into several different types of healing modalities such as Reiki energy healing and Emotional Freedom Techniques (EFT), also known as tapping. Actively engaging in the process of healing has been an empowering endeavor, which involved persistence and consistency in reclaiming agency over my life.

For years, the echoes of my disheartening childhood and unfulfilled adult aspirations have cast shadows on my path through life. In my golden years of restlessness and yearning for change, a newfound sense of purpose emerged. As I sifted through the shattered pieces of my past experiences, I unearthed hidden treasures nestled within the deep cracks of my broken inner landscape where my history waited for healing and transformation. These treasures were more than fragments of insights. They were profound seeds of wisdom waiting to be embraced and shared with the world.

I soon recognized and realized that I had stumbled upon the unexpected benefits of unlocking treasure chests of gifts within five areas of life. This powerful discovery led to the birth of the five golden keys, which brought about a newfound sense of purpose, joy, and fulfillment in my life and the lives of others that have been touched by the evolution of the G.I.F.T.S. method thanks to its profound synergy and powerful ripple effect.

Let's briefly explore some of the benefits of embracing these gifts before delving deeper into their transformative power in the chapters that follow.

Gratitude

Gratitude sets the stage for you, inviting you to cultivate a mindset of abundance and profound appreciation for the blessings in your life. It serves as your unwavering North Star. It's a guiding light that not only illuminates your journey, it also empowers you to navigate challenges with grace and unwavering humility. Grounded in the present moment, gratitude allows you to savor the beauty of each day, even amidst life's uncertainties, fostering a deep sense of connection to the world around you. It's more than just an emotion or a practice; it's a way of being that enriches every interaction, deepens relationships, and fortifies your resilience in the face of adversity.

With gratitude as your compass, each day becomes infused with profound meaning and purpose, as you embrace the goodness that surrounds you and embark on a journey of growth and fulfillment.

Intuitive Intention

Intuition is a fundamental aspect of human experience. We are all born with innate intuition that develops over time. Innate intuition is a natural gift, an inherent ability within each of us to tap into our inner wisdom and instincts. Living with intuitive intention means tapping into your inner wisdom and trusting your instincts to guide your actions, thoughts, and behaviors. It's about recognizing and listening to those subtle cues from your intuition rather than solely relying on rational thinking to set specific goals or outcomes.

When you embrace intuitive intention, you're charting a course for your life based on what feels authentic to you. You become the architect of your destiny, paving the way for greater fulfillment and purpose. By clarifying your intuitive intentions and identifying what truly resonates with your soul, you create a roadmap for your life. This heightened awareness allows you to make more focused and deliberate choices, aligning yourself with paths that nourish your spirit and bring you joy.

Living with intuitive intention empowers you to make decisions that are in harmony with your authentic self, prioritizing activities and relationships that enrich your life. When your actions are guided by intuitive intention, you experience a sense of coherence and harmony. You feel more grounded and centered, knowing that you're living in alignment with your deepest values and aspirations.

Ultimately, embracing intuitive intention and tapping into it brings a profound sense of fulfillment and purpose, allowing you to lead a life that feels meaningful and true to who you are in every moment.

Family and Friends

Your relationships with your family and friends play a pivotal role in maintaining your mental and emotional balance. These connections are lifelines. They offer guidance, support, and deep nurturing bonds that enrich your life in countless ways. First and foremost, your loved ones provide a sense of belonging and connection. They are your companions through life's ups and downs, offering a shoulder to lean on and a listening ear when you need it most. Their presence brings comfort and reassurance, reminding you that you are never alone. In times of struggle or uncertainty, your family and friends can offer invaluable guidance and wisdom. They can share their perspectives and experiences to help you navigate life's challenges with greater clarity and insight. Whether it's a word of encouragement or a piece of advice, their support can make all the difference in helping you find your way.

But perhaps most importantly, your relationships are a source of love and warmth that nourishes your soul when the bonds you share with them are built on a foundation of trust and mutual respect, creating a space where you can be your truest self without judgment or rejection. In nurturing these relationships, you cultivate a sense of belonging and connection that is essential for your mental and emotional well-being. You feel supported and uplifted upon knowing that you have a network of people who genuinely care about your happiness and success.

Ultimately, your relationships with your family and friends bring joy, meaning, and fulfillment to your life. They are the threads that weave together the fabric of your existence, creating a tapestry of love and connection that sustains you through every season of life.

Treasured Wisdom

The treasure trove of knowledge and wisdom you process holds a unique power in fostering personal growth and self-discovery through profound personal reflection. Wisdom is a gentle nudge from within the urges you to delve deep into your innermost thoughts and feelings and explore the depths of your being. When you engage in personal reflection guided by the things you treasure, you embark on a journey of self-discovery. You begin to uncover your passions, values, and core principles. Your treasured wisdom becomes those guiding lights that illuminate your path in life. It's like peeling back the layers of an onion, revealing the essence of who you truly are.

As you reflect on your experiences, beliefs, and aspirations, you gain a deeper understanding of yourself and your place in the world. You become more attuned to your inner voice and you learn to trust your instincts and intuition. This newfound self-awareness empowers you to make choices that align with your authentic self, leading to a lifestyle that is in harmony with your deepest desires and values. Treasured wisdom encourages you to embrace your uniqueness and celebrate your individuality. It's about honoring your strengths and embracing your weaknesses, recognizing that each aspect of yourself contributes your life. By embracing your authenticity, you open yourself up to a world of possibilities and potential.

Ultimately, treasured wisdom is a catalyst for growth and transformation. It challenges you to step outside of your comfort zone and explore new horizons. It invites you to embrace change and the journey of self-discovery, knowing that every experience is an opportunity for growth and learning. It empowers you to live a life that is true to yourself, a life filled with purpose, passion, and authenticity. It's a journey of self-discovery that leads to a deeper sense of fulfillment and meaning, allowing you to shine brightly as the unique individual you were meant to be.

Self-love & Care

Self-love & care serve as the cornerstone of a healthy and fulfilling life, providing the foundational support upon which all else is built. When you prioritize self-love and care, you prioritize your well-being in every aspect—physically, mentally, emotionally, and spiritually. It's about recognizing your worth and treating yourself with the kindness and compassion you deserve. By emphasizing routines that promote comprehensive well-being, you deeply invest in yourself. You make choices that nourish your body, mind, and soul, ensuring that you have the energy and vitality to live life to the fullest.

Self-love and care also involve setting boundaries and saying no when necessary. It's about honoring your needs and respecting your limits by knowing that you can't pour from an empty cup. When prioritizing your well-being, you create space for growth and abundance in all areas of your life. Nurturing yourself is not selfish, it's essential. When you take care of yourself, you show up as the best version of yourself in all your roles and relationships. You're more resilient in the face of challenges and better equipped to handle whatever life throws your way.

Ultimately, self-love and care are the keys to unlocking a life of joy, fulfillment, and purpose. They empower you to thrive, both personally and professionally, and create a life that reflects your deepest desires and aspirations. So go ahead and prioritize yourself. You're worth it!

Embracing The G.I.F.T.S. Method

The G.I.F.T.S. method is a unified system designed to empower you to uncover the habits and mindsets that will truly transform your life in a meaningful way. It goes beyond quick fixes and temporary solutions to create lasting change from the inside out. With the G.I.F.T.S. method, you'll learn to cultivate positive habits and mindsets that lead to a more balanced, purpose-driven, and joyous existence. As such, this roadmap guides you toward a fulfilling and authentic life.

Whether you're looking to improve your relationships, find more meaning in your work, or simply live with more joy and vitality, the G.I.F.T.S. method can help. It's a comprehensive approach that addresses key aspects of your life, giving you the tools and support you need to thrive. I invite you to step into your power and create the life you've always dreamed of. I am here to support you every step of the way. It's time to unlock your full potential and live a life that truly brings you joy and fulfillment.

Imagine waking up each day to a life where you are truly seen, heard, respected, and acknowledged for the wonderful person you are. Picture yourself radiating with positive energy and sending out ripples of warmth and kindness that touch the lives of everyone you encounter. In this life, you possess the power to create a truly gratifying and purposeful existence. It's a life where love flows freely, where every experience is an opportunity for growth and learning, and where heartfelt connections with others enrich your journey. Just imagine the possibilities that lie before you when you embrace your true self and live authentically.

You can shape your reality and create a world where love and compassion reign supreme with every smile you share, every kind word you speak, and every act of generosity you extend can help make this world a better place. These are the building blocks of the life you've always dreamed of. And within you, deep in your heart and soul, lies the potential to turn that dream into a beautiful reality. So don't hold back. Let your light shine brightly for all to see.

As you unlock and embrace each of the five golden keys within the G.I.F.T.S. method, you'll begin to see positive changes unfold in your life. Like flowers blooming in the garden of your soul, the gifts of self-awareness, fulfillment, and purpose will blossom and flourish. You'll cultivate a life rich in love while learning and gaining meaningful connections with others. Within you lies the power to create a gratifying and purposeful well-lived life that leaves a legacy of heartfelt connections and admiration.

Embrace the love and joy that surrounds you. Let it guide you toward a life filled with purpose, fulfillment, and heartfelt connections. The world is waiting for you to step into your greatness, and the possibilities are endless.

*"The practice of forgiveness
is our most important contribution
to the healing of the world."
– Marianne Williamson*

KEY OF GRATITUDE

Unlock the gift of appreciating the blessings in your life by cultivating a positive mindset. Through the daily practice of focusing on the positives, you shift your perspective by embracing the healing potential of positive thinking, which in turn radiates positivity and gratitude to those around you.

7

The Powerful Gift of Appreciation

When you consciously acknowledge and appreciate the good things around you like a beautiful sunset, a kind gesture from a friend, or even the warmth of the sun on your skin, you start to see the world through a different lens. Problems that once seemed insurmountable now appear as opportunities for growth and learning. Gratitude is a fundamental element that contributes to a sense of balance, well-being, and fulfillment. Take a look at some of the benefits:

- Gratitude shifts your mindset from scarcity to abundance,
- Enhances mental well-being by reducing stress and anxiety,
- Fosters happiness and life satisfaction,
- Strengthens relationships by deepening connections and promoting empathy,
- Acts as a powerful tool for resilience that will help you navigate adversity with grace and optimism,
- Promotes mindful living by encouraging the savoring of present moments,
- Stimulates the production of feel-good neurotransmitters like dopamine and serotonin,

- Improves sleep quality and duration,
- Boosts immune function and overall physical health,
- Enhances emotional regulation and reduces symptoms of depression,
- Increases self-esteem and overall sense of well-being,
- Improves cognitive function and enhances brain health,
- Cultivates a positive outlook and mindset, leading to greater optimism,
- Promotes socialization and acts of kindness towards others,
- and creates a ripple effect of positivity in your life and the lives of those around you.

I have many blessings in my life, which I am deeply thankful for beyond words. You often hear sayings like "count your blessings", "focus on the positives", and "have an attitude of gratitude." The key to unlocking the gifts of gratitude is appreciating the blessings in your life and cultivating a positive mindset. Through daily gratitude practice, you can shift your perspective by embracing the healing potential of positive thinking, much like affirmations, which in turn radiates positivity as gratitude extends to those around you.

But what if you're hurting? In moments of struggle and despair, the idea of expressing gratitude can feel like an impossible, insurmountable task despite all the other blessings in your life. During challenging times, feeling grateful isn't always easy. The complexities of life can overshadow your ability to recognize the good around you.

Know this: gratitude doesn't require you to ignore pain or dismiss your struggles. Instead, it invites you to find moments of light amid the darkness, appreciate small victories, and extend compassion to yourself during difficult times. By embracing gratitude with authenticity you acknowledge the validity of your struggles and choose to use gratitude as a guiding light toward healing and growth.

Discovering Silver Linings

When intense emotions like sadness, grief, or anxiety overwhelm you, gratitude may not come to mind. In moments of profound loss or crisis, your reality may feel shattered. The weight of your feelings can consume all your mental and emotional energy. Simply getting through the day can feel like an immense challenge, leaving little room for positive thoughts like gratitude.

During times of deep distress, it's important to allow yourself to experience all your emotions without guilt. Feeling overwhelmed doesn't diminish your appreciation for the positive aspects of your life or the love from those around you. Give yourself the grace and space to navigate through your emotions without self-judgment.

Even in tough times, there's a silver lining hidden behind the clouds like a small glimmer of hope, a meaningful connection, or a valuable lesson that helps you grow. Challenges can often open doors to discoveries and growth when you trust in your strength to get through the dark times. Even a flicker of gratitude can be a guiding light that brings peace back into your life.

Discovering silver linings means noticing unexpected positives from difficult situations such as growing stronger, feeling closer to loved ones, or learning important life lessons. It's not about ignoring the hard stuff. It's about choosing to focus on the rays of light that peek through the darkness, leading you to brighter days ahead. Looking for silver linings is a choice you make, a reminder that hope is always there and waiting for you to notice it.

Personal Story: *A Pivotal Moment*

While driving my camper van along tree-lined roads, I felt a familiar mix of excitement and loneliness. For nearly three years, I'd been embarking on solo trips where I explored new places and met like-minded people. At first, these adventures thrilled me, offering a stark contrast to the routine of home life.

But as the novelty wore off, a persistent sadness crept in. I couldn't shake the disappointment of not sharing these experiences with my husband. While I respected his preference for routine, and his interest in golfing with buddies and quiet evenings at home, I yearned for more. The older I got, the more I wanted to live life to the fullest. With his blessings and the encouragement of our children who said, "Mom, if dad doesn't want to go, go yourself," I started traveling solo.

I pulled my camper van into the forest to find a camping spot among other summer campers. The forest had become my happy place. I cherished gazing up at the tall trees while listening to songbirds, watching chipmunks play, and savoring the aroma of a campfire. I parked among the tall trees. The peaceful setting usually soothed me. But tonight, it only amplified my inner turmoil. I felt as if I was living a double life: the adventurous traveler and the homebody wife, with an ever-widening gap between the two.

As night fell, the silence forced me to confront the issues I'd been avoiding. Spending all this time alone had turned into a soul-searching journey, unearthing unresolved feelings from my childhood now took center stage.

"Why can't I move past this?" I asked myself, tired of rehashing old pain. I knew my current sadness wasn't just about travel fatigue or missing my husband. This nomadic lifestyle had become a mirror, reflecting the complex emotions I'd carried for years.

As I gazed at the starry sky, I realized this journey was forcing me to confront my past in ways I hadn't anticipated. The feelings of being unseen and undervalued as a child resurfaced with startling clarity. Despite the years that had passed, these wounds still felt raw. I wondered how these old hurts were shaping my present, influencing my need for adventure and my struggle with solitude. My path had been leading me, not just to new destinations, it's also to a deeper understanding of myself and the childhood experiences that I had molded me.

Reflecting on My Journey

Throughout my life, I have periodically sought to heal my inner child by exploring various healing modalities, including Reiki energy healing and Emotional Freedom Techniques (EFT), also known as tapping. While these methods provided some relief, it was only temporary. I had not yet discovered the power of gratitude. I wrestled with feelings of self-pity followed by the guilt I felt when comparing my struggles to those who faced greater hardship.

Embracing genuine gratitude hasn't come easily to me. Resentment, shame, guilt, and fear, coupled with negative thought patterns and distorted perceptions, had kept me trapped in a cycle of negativity about my upbringing for most of my life. The scars of my childhood cast a thick veil of darkness over any potential rays of hope, making it difficult for me to find the silver linings.

Yet, as I spent time in the forest, studying and considering the power of gratitude as a possible way to better understand the complexities of my past, it led me to a surprising discovery; empathy. I began to realize that my parents faced challenges and responsibilities that were difficult for them to manage. My inclination to appear self-reliant, as a way to avoid adding to the chaos around me, may have unintentionally conveyed to them that I required less attention.

This newfound empathy prompted me to notice valuable lessons. By being self-reliant, I learned the importance of independence and resilience. I began to understand that my parents did the best they could with the tools and knowledge they had. Recognizing their struggles and limitations helped me see them in a more compassionate light.

At the same time, I became aware of the self-inflicted damage I caused due to my low self-esteem. My negative self-perception led me to make choices that reinforced my feelings of unworthiness. I realize now that I didn't know how to self-parent. While it's not my fault, I must take responsibility for my actions. Understanding this has allowed me to forgive myself and approach my healing with more kindness and patience. This journey has taught me the importance of nurturing my inner child and providing myself with the love and support I always needed.

By acknowledging both my parents' efforts and my missteps, I have been able to move forward with a greater sense of clarity and purpose, embracing the lessons learned along the way.

Initially, I wavered between acknowledging the pain of my past and embracing the silver linings as gifts emerging from the shadows. Actively engaging in this healing process is an empowering endeavor that requires persistence and consistency to reclaim agency over my life. Though the scars have faded, some of the impacts still linger, and twinges of it can be triggered by stress. But each step forward is a testament to my resilience and determination to rewrite the narratives that no longer serve me.

The Healing Power of Gratitude

The power of gratitude cannot be overstated. It has the potential to transform pain into growth. Practicing gratitude not only helps foster a greater sense of appreciation for the present moment but also fosters a deeper connection with yourself, others and the world around you.

During life's challenges and uncertainties, it's easy to feel overwhelmed by stress, consumed by anxiety, or weighed down by depression. Stress has become an unavoidable part of

life, with its relentless demands and pressures taking a toll on our physical and mental health. However, research has shown that practicing gratitude can act as a powerful shield against stress, helping to reduce its harmful effects on our bodies and minds.

By focusing on the things you are thankful for, you can shift your attention away from stressors and towards the blessings in your life, creating a buffer against their damaging effects.

Anxiety can be a crippling condition that traps us in a cycle of worry and fear that can rob us of our peace of mind. Yet, studies have found that gratitude can be a potent antidote to anxiety to calm it's racing thoughts and soothe frazzled nerves.

Depression can cast a dark shadow over our lives, enveloping us in a fog of hopelessness and despair. However, research has also shown that gratitude has the power to pierce through this as well as offer a glimmer of light and hope to those struggling with depression. By focusing on the things you are grateful for, you can reframe your perspective and find reasons to keep going, even in the darkest of times.

Gratitude acts as a reminder that even in your darkest moments, there is still beauty and goodness to be found in the world. It is a powerful tool that you can use to reshape your thought patterns toward positivity. While practicing gratitude and emphasizing the positive aspects of life can be powerful tools for well-being, it's equally vital to acknowledge the reality that, at times, we all experience negativity.

The constant pursuit of positivity, especially prevalent in social media, can inadvertently create a facade of an idealized life. Most of us tend to share our triumphs and joys on platforms like Facebook and Instagram. But, what about the inevitable challenges and moments of vulnerability?

For instance, consider the meticulously curated social media feeds where every image exudes happiness and success. Yet we all know that behind the scenes, real life unfolds with its share of difficulties, disappointments, and moments of self-doubt. Failing to acknowledge, suppress, and ignore these feelings by unplugging them from reality contributes to internal conflict and a sense of isolation. Pretending to be happy and grateful when you are not is like wearing a mask that doesn't quite fit. It's uncomfortable, and it doesn't allow for genuine connections.

Whereas we don't want or need to air our dirty laundry or contribute to online hate, practicing genuine gratitude can have profound benefits for our mental health and well-being. No one enjoys reading or listening to hate-filled content online, which underscores the importance of spreading positivity instead. But by cultivating authentic gratitude, we can strengthen our ability to form meaningful connections both offline and online.

Plus, like affirmations, gratitude stimulates the production of feel-good neurotransmitters like dopamine and serotonin, which are essential for regulating mood and promoting overall mental wellness. It's like giving your brain a daily dose of happiness vitamins. I find it so interesting to note that we can train our brain to rewire itself for positivity through affirmations and practicing gratitude.

Gratitude and the Brain

Gratitude has been a subject of fascination not only for philosophers and spiritual leaders but also for neuroscientists seeking to understand the intricate workings of the brain and its profound impact on well-being. Let's take a look behind the scenes:

Through research, scientists uncovered connections between gratitude and various regions of the brain, shedding light on the neural pathways that shape our mindset and contribute to a balanced, and fulfilling life. Gratitude is a powerful tool you can use for your mental well-being. By understanding the brain's response to gratitude, you can leverage and harness its power to improve your emotional health, build resilience, and create a more fulfilling life.

The connection between gratitude and the brain is closely linked. When you express gratitude, your brain releases feel-good hormones like dopamine and serotonin. Dopamine is responsible for feelings of pleasure, excitement, and happiness, whereas serotonin has more to do with feelings of satisfaction, contentment, and overall well-being. Regularly practicing gratitude can help increase these hormone levels, which in turn activates a cascade of physiological effects, including the release of oxytocin.

Oxytocin, often referred to as the "love hormone," fosters social bonding, trust, and feelings of connection. Gratitude allows us to find the strength within ourselves to cultivate a positive mindset. This in turn makes us less likely to become overwhelmed by negative events or experiences and be more capable of navigating the challenges of life. In simple terms, this complex network in your brain is where emotions are regulated.

Research suggests that practicing gratitude can lead to structural changes in the region associated with memory and learning. The strength and growth of these neural connections are linked to an improved ability to adapt to new information and experiences. As gratitude becomes a habit, it shapes the emotional landscape in this network, contributing to an increased capacity for positive emotional experiences and emotional resilience.

Gratitude, much like any skill, can be cultivated and refined through consistent practice. Training your brain is about sculpting neural pathways that predispose you to a more positive and grateful mindset. These intricate networks of interconnected neurons in your brain; known as neural pathways play a crucial role in the formation of your habits and your behaviors. Repeated gratitude experiences, over time, can strengthen and reinforce your neural pathways, making gratitude your natural response.

Neuroplasticity is the brain's ability to adapt and reorganize itself. It is at the heart of this process. Understanding the neuroscience of gratitude paints a vivid picture of how your neural architecture responds to the practice of appreciation for cultivating a balanced, fulfilling life.

By actively engaging in practices that stimulate these brain regions and pathways, you empower yourself to navigate challenges with resilience, savor positive experiences, and foster a mindset that nurtures your overall well-being. At the same time, it weeds out negativity.

In the next chapter, we'll delve into practical exercises aimed at training your brain to cultivate positivity and resilience through gratitude. These exercises will deepen your awareness and appreciation of gratitude in your life, helping you build a more positive outlook and mindset.

"When we focus on our gratitude, the tide of disappointment goes out and the tide of love rushes in. Gratitude brings peace for today and creates a vision for tomorrow, making our hearts light and our spirits high."
– Kristin Armstrong

8

Cultivating a Gratitude Practice

In the journey of personal growth and resilience, gratitude serves as a powerful tool that allows us to train our minds toward positivity and appreciation, even in the face of challenges. The exercises in this chapter are designed to help you develop a deeper awareness of gratitude in your daily life.

By consistently engaging in these exercises, you will strengthen your ability to notice and appreciate the positive aspects of your experiences, no matter how small. Over time, these practices will nurture a more positive outlook and empower you to navigate life with greater resilience and joy.

Whether you're new to gratitude practices or looking to deepen your existing routine, these exercises offer a pathway to harness the transformative power of gratitude. Let's embark on this journey together and cultivate a mindset that fosters fulfillment, resilience, and authentic well-being.

Consider this. When you consciously acknowledge and appreciate the good things around you like the beauty of a sunset, a kind gesture from a friend, or the warmth of the sun on your skin, you begin to see the world through a different lens. Challenges that once felt overwhelming now appear as opportunities for growth and learning. Research has shown that expressing gratitude boosts feelings of happiness and contentment. By intentionally practicing gratitude, you can strengthen your brain's neural pathways to filter out negativity and replace it with positivity.

Focusing on the positive aspects of your experiences shifts your mindset, enhances your mental well-being, strengthens your relationships, fosters resilience, and promotes mindful living. This shift in perspective improves your overall attitude, fostering a more optimistic outlook on life.

Expressing appreciation deepens your connections with others and strengthens the bonds of friendship and love. A simple thank you or a heartfelt expression of gratitude can uplift spirits and foster trust, understanding, and intimacy in your relationships. This ripple effect of gratitude can spread far and wide, enriching not only your life but also the lives of those around you.

The Foundation for Cultivating Gratitude

In pursuit of cultivating gratitude and embracing a more fulfilling life, it's essential to establish a strong foundation of self-care and healthy living. These practices lay the groundwork for emotional regulation, resilience, and overall well-being, making them vital components of your journey toward gratitude. Let's explore how prioritizing regular sleep, nutrition, and exercise can enhance your capacity to experience and express gratitude.

Regular Sleep

Adequate and quality sleep is a cornerstone of emotional regulation and cognitive function. When you're well-rested, your brain's limbic system functions optimally, allowing you to process emotions more effectively. Sleep deprivation can hinder your ability to appreciate positive experiences and maintain a balanced perspective. By prioritizing restful sleep, you create a fertile ground for nurturing gratitude and emotional well-being.

Nutrition

A balanced diet directly impacts brain health and emotional stability. Consuming nutrient-dense foods rich in omega-3 fatty acids, antioxidants, and essential vitamins supports cognitive function and mood regulation. These nutrients play a role in neurotransmitter production, that would then influence+ your ability to experience positive emotions and resilience. Eating mindfully and nourishing your body contribute to a heightened sense of well-being, fostering receptivity to gratitude.

Exercise

Physical activity is a natural mood enhancer and stress reliever. Engaging in regular exercise promotes the release of endorphins, which elevate mood and reduce anxiety. By incorporating movement into your daily routine, you can enhance your emotional resilience and capacity for gratitude. Exercise also fosters a deeper mind-body connection, facilitating mindfulness and presence in your experiences.

By prioritizing self-care practices such as regular sleep, balanced nutrition, and physical activity, you fortify your emotional foundation for embracing gratitude. These practices cultivate a harmonious relationship between mind and body, allowing you to approach life's challenges with greater resilience and positivity.

As you embark on gratitude exercises and mindfulness techniques, let's integrate these mind and body principles to optimize your well-being and deepen your appreciation for life's blessings.

Mind and Body Principles

Navigating through difficult emotions and embarking on a gratitude journey can be deeply personal and sometimes challenging. Here are some foundational steps to nurture and support your well-being as you begin this transformative process:

1. **Acknowledge Your Feelings**

    Allow yourself to acknowledge and validate your feelings without judgment. It's okay to feel overwhelmed, lost, or hopeless at times. Recognizing your emotions is the first step toward self-compassion and healing.

2. **Start Small**

    Begin by noticing small moments of brightness amidst the darkness. Look for simple joys like a warm cup of tea, a gentle breeze, or the sound of rain. These small moments serve as beacons of hope and can gradually expand your capacity for gratitude.

3. **Practice Self-Compassion**

    Treat yourself with kindness and understanding during challenging times. Practice self-compassion by offering yourself words of encouragement and comfort. Remember, it's okay if gratitude feels out of reach right now.

4. **Seek Support**

    You don't have to face this journey alone. Reach out to trusted friends, family members, or a therapist for support. Surround yourself with people who uplift and encourage you alongside those who provide a sense of connection and solidarity.

5. **Focus on Moments of Grace**

   Even amidst hardship, moments of grace exist—acts of kindness, gestures of love, or peaceful reflections. Pay attention to these moments and fully appreciate their significance in your life.

6. **Cultivate Hope**

   Hold onto hope and trust in the possibility of brighter days ahead. Believe in the resilience of your spirit and the potential for growth through challenges. Cultivating hope can sustain you through difficult times.

Remember, this journey requires courage and patience. Take one step at a time and honor your unique path toward healing and gratitude. You are not alone. Embrace the support around you and trust in your inner strength to guide you forward.

> *"The real gift of gratitude is that the more grateful you are, the more present you become."* ~ Robert Holden

Practical Exercises for Transformation

Now that you've laid the groundwork for nurturing your well-being, let's explore practical gratitude exercises to cultivate positivity and resilience in your life. These exercises are designed to help you embrace gratitude as a daily practice and harness its profound benefits. Choose one or more exercises that resonate with you from this list and begin incorporating them into your routine.

Embrace these exercises as tools and practices with an open heart and observe the transformative impact of gratitude on your mindset and well-being. Remember, the journey of gratitude begins with a single step. Start today and nurture a mindset of abundance and appreciation.

Gratitude Journaling

Dedicate a few minutes each day to write down things you're grateful for. Reflect on positive experiences, meaningful connections, or moments of joy. Writing in a gratitude journal can shift your focus toward appreciation. See the Three Blessings exercise below for information on adding this to your journal.

Expressing Gratitude

Reach out to someone you appreciate and express your gratitude. Send a heartfelt message, make a phone call, or write a letter. Sharing gratitude strengthens relationships and fosters connection. See the Gratitude Letter Writing and Random Acts of Kindness exercise below for information on implementing this exercise.

The Three Blessings

The Three Blessings exercise is a simple yet powerful gratitude practice designed to cultivate a positive mindset and foster a sense of appreciation for the blessings in your life. Rooted in positive psychology, this exercise encourages you to reflect on and acknowledge the positive aspects of your daily experiences. By regularly engaging in this practice, it can enhance your overall well-being, resilience, and your outlook on life.

1. **Choose a Time:** Set aside a few minutes each day for this exercise. Many people find it best to do this either in the morning to start the day on a positive note or in the evening to reflect on the day's events.

2. **Reflect:** Take a moment to reflect on your day and identify three things that you feel grateful for or things that went well. These can be simple pleasures, moments of kindness, achievements, or

any other positive experiences.

3. **Write Them Down:** Write down your three blessings in a journal, notebook, or even on your phone or computer. Writing them down helps solidify them in your mind and allows you to revisit them later.

4. **Be Specific:** When listing your blessings, try to be as specific as possible. Instead of simply writing, "I'm grateful for my family," you might write, "I'm grateful for the laughter shared with my family during dinner tonight."

5. **Reflect on Why:** For each blessing, take a moment to reflect on why it was meaningful to you. What about that experience or moment that brought you joy, satisfaction, or gratitude? Consider sharing your thoughts with someone you trust.

6. **Repeat Daily:** Make the Three Blessings exercise a daily habit. Consistency is key to reaping the full benefits of this practice. Over time, you may find that you naturally start to notice and appreciate more positive aspects of your life.

Examples:

1. *Today, during our team meeting, I had a constructive and positive conversation with Sarah. We brainstormed ideas, and her encouragement made me feel valued and motivated.*

   I appreciate Sarah's collaborative spirit and how she fosters a positive work environment. Her feedback and support make our teamwork enjoyable and productive.

2. *This morning, I woke up early and decided to go for a walk. The sunrise was breathtaking, casting warm hues across the sky. It reminded me of the beauty in simple moments.*

   Nature has a remarkable way of bringing peace and tranquility. The sunrise reminded me to slow down, be present, and find joy in the small wonders around me.

3. *I received an unexpected call from my friend, Alex, who wanted to check in and chat. His support and genuine interest in my well-being lifted my spirits and made my day.*

   Alex's call showed me the importance of genuine connections. His thoughtful questions and encouragement reinforced the value of strong friendships.

Reflection:
Reflect on your entries. Do you notice any patterns or themes in what you appreciate? Begin to share one gratitude daily with someone you trust.

Sharing my gratitude with Sarah and Alex enhanced our connections.

This exercise helped me focus on the positive aspects of my day, even during challenging moments.

Gratitude Jar

A gratitude jar is a tangible and visually impactful way to cultivate a mindset of gratitude and appreciation in your daily life. It involves writing down moments, experiences, or things that you are thankful for and then storing them in a jar or container. Over time, the jar becomes filled with these expressions of gratitude, serving as a reminder of the abundance of blessings in your life. The purpose of a gratitude jar is to shift focus towards the positive aspects of life, foster feelings of contentment, and promote overall well-being.

1. **Select a Jar:** Choose a jar, container, or box that you find visually appealing and that can comfortably hold slips of paper. Consider decorating the jar to make it feel more personal and inviting.

2. **Prepare Supplies:** Gather supplies such as small pieces of paper, pens, markers, and scissors. These will be used to write down moments of gratitude to place in the jar.

3. **Identify Gratitude Moments:** Throughout the day, be mindful of moments, experiences, or things that you are thankful for. These could be anything from a kind gesture from a friend to a beautiful sunset.

4. **Write Them Down:** Take a piece of paper and write down one thing you are grateful for on each slip. Be specific and descriptive to capture the essence of the moment.

5. **Fold and Add to the Jar:** Fold the slip of paper and place it in the gratitude jar. Repeat this process daily or as often as you like.

6. **Reflect and Revisit:** Periodically, take time to reflect on the contents of the gratitude jar. Read through the slips of paper and revisit the moments of gratitude you have recorded. Allow

yourself to savor the positive emotions associated with each one.

7. **Continue the Practice:** Keep the gratitude jar prominently displayed in a place where you will see it regularly. Continue adding to it over time, and watch as it fills up with expressions of gratitude and appreciation.

Gratitude Jar with a Twist

Instead of a traditional gratitude jar, consider creating a "gratitude tree" or "gratitude board" where you can hang or pin your notes of gratitude. This visual representation can serve as a constant reminder of the abundance of blessings in your life. By implementing a gratitude jar, tree, or board into your daily life, you can cultivate a greater sense of gratitude, positivity, and mindfulness. This would lead to a more fulfilling and enriched existence.

Gratitude Walk

A gratitude walk is a mindful practice that involves immersing yourself in the present moment while walking and consciously focusing on feelings of gratitude and appreciation. It offers an opportunity for you to connect with nature or the environment around you while cultivating a sense of gratitude for the beauty and abundance you feel and see in the world. This practice can be deeply calming, rejuvenating, and uplifting. It can provide you with a refreshing perspective on the blessings in your life.

1. **Choose a Location:** Select a location for your gratitude walk that allows you to connect with nature or one that simply offers a serene environment conducive to reflection. This could be a park, a nature trail, a beach, or even just around your

neighborhood.

2. **Set Your Intention:** Before you begin walking, take a moment to set your intention for the walk. Decide to focus on feelings of gratitude and appreciation for the duration of your walk.

3. **Begin Walking Mindfully:** Start walking at a comfortable pace and pay attention to each step you take. Notice the crunch of the gravel beneath your feet or the soft cushion of grass as it welcomes each step.

4. **Engage Your Senses:** As you walk, inhale deeply and allow the crisp, fresh air to fill your lungs, perhaps catching the earthy scent of soil or the floral aroma of blooming plants.

    Take in the vibrant hues of the landscape, the verdant greens of the trees, the brilliant splashes of color from wildflowers, and the warm golden glow of the sun.

    Listen intently to the symphony of nature unfolding around you. Hear the melodic songs of birds, the gentle rustling of leaves in the breeze, and the soothing cadence of a nearby stream or fountain.

    Reach out and feel the smooth bark of a tree trunk or the delicate petals of a flower. Notice the temperature of the air against your skin and the gentle caress of the wind on your face.

    As you walk, allow your senses to fully immerse you in the present moment. Notice how the sensations of your surroundings evoke feelings of wonder, serenity, and deep appreciation. Let these embodied experiences of gratitude guide your steps.

5. **Focus on Gratitude:** With each step, consciously turn your attention to things you are grateful for. Allow yourself to fully experience feelings of gratitude for these blessings. By engaging all your senses, you can deepen your connection to the natural world and cultivate a profound sense of appreciation for the beauty that surrounds you. Each step becomes an opportunity to savor the richness of the present moment.

6. **Practice Presence:** If your mind starts to wander or become distracted, gently bring your focus back to the present moment and your intention of gratitude. Let go of any worries or concerns and immerse yourself fully in the experience of the walk.

7. **Reflect:** Towards the end of your walk, take a few moments to reflect on your experience. Notice how you feel after focusing on gratitude during your walk. Take note of any insights or feelings of peace and contentment that arise.

8. **Express Gratitude:** Before concluding your walk, take a moment to express gratitude for the opportunity to connect with nature and experience moments of beauty and abundance.

Incorporating gratitude into your walks can transform them into nourishing and enriching experiences that contribute to your overall well-being. Practice gratitude walks regularly to cultivate a deeper sense of appreciation for the world around you and the blessings in your life.

Gratitude Letters

Gratitude letters are heartfelt expressions of appreciation and thanks that you can write to people who have positively impacted your life in some way. The letters you write to others can serve as meaningful gestures of gratitude that convey your genuine appreciation for their kindness, support, or influence. You cam acknowledge their impact on you that you appreciate. Whether you send a gratitude letter via mail or you deliver it in person, your gratitude letters have the power to strengthen your relationships, uplift spirits, and foster a culture of appreciation and connection that will have a ripple effect. By taking the time to express your heartfelt gratitude to others, you have the power to transform lives and deepen the connections that matter to you.

1. **Select Recipients:** Begin by identifying individuals whom you would like to express gratitude towards. They could be family members, friends, mentors, colleagues, teachers, or anyone else who has positively influenced your life.

2. **Reflect on Impact:** Take some time to reflect on the specific ways in which each individual has made a difference in your life. Consider the kindness they have shown, the support they have provided, or the valuable lessons they have imparted.

3. **Write from the Heart:** Sit down with pen and paper or go to your computer and begin drafting your gratitude letter. Write from the heart. Express genuine appreciation and thanks for the impact the recipient has had on you. Be specific and heartfelt in your expression of gratitude.

4. **Include Specific Examples:** Share specific examples or anecdotes that illustrate the impact the recipient has had on your life. This helps to personalize the letter and convey the depth of your gratitude.

5. **Express Sincerity:** Be sincere and genuine in your expression of gratitude. Avoid exaggeration or insincerity and focus on

expressing your true feelings of appreciation and thanks.

6. **Be Concise and Clear:** Keep your letter concise and to the point, while still conveying your gratitude in a meaningful way. Aim for clarity and coherence in your writing.

7. **Deliver the Letter:** Once you have finished writing your gratitude letter, decide how you would like to deliver it. You can choose to send it via mail, deliver it in person, or even read it aloud to the recipient.

By incorporating gratitude letters into your life, you can strengthen relationships, foster positivity, and spread joy and appreciation to those who have made a positive difference in your life.

Random Acts of Kindness

Random acts of kindness involve intentionally performing small, unexpected gestures of generosity or compassion towards others without expecting anything in return. These acts can take many forms, from holding the door open for someone to paying for a stranger's coffee or offering a kind word to someone in need. Random acts of kindness have the power to brighten someone's day, spread positivity, and create a ripple effect of kindness in the world.

1. **Be Observant:** Pay attention to opportunities for acts of kindness in your daily life. These opportunities can arise at any moment, whether you're at home, at work, or out in the community.

2. **Start Small:** Begin by performing small acts of kindness that are easy to incorporate into your daily routine. This could include smiling at strangers, holding the door open, or offering a

compliment to someone.

3. **Be Genuine:** Approach acts of kindness with sincerity and authenticity. Let your actions come from a genuine desire to brighten someone's day and make a positive impact.

4. **Step Outside Your Comfort Zone:** Challenge yourself to step outside your comfort zone and perform acts of kindness that may require a bit more effort or courage. This could involve volunteering your time, offering assistance to someone in need, or initiating a conversation with a stranger.

5. **Spread Positivity:** Encourage others to join you in spreading kindness by sharing your experiences and inspiring others to perform their own acts of kindness.

6. **Practice Regularly:** Make acts of kindness a regular part of your life by incorporating them into your daily routine. Set a goal to perform at least one act of kindness each day or week.

7. **Reflect on the Impact:** Take time to reflect on the impact of your acts of kindness. Notice how they make you feel and the positive reactions they elicit from others. Celebrate the difference you are making in the lives of those around you.

8. **Pay It Forward:** Encourage recipients of your kindness to pay it forward by performing their acts of kindness for others as well. By creating a ripple effect of kindness, you can amplify the positive impact of your actions.

By incorporating random acts of kindness into your daily life, you can spread joy, foster connection, and contribute to a more compassionate and caring world.

*"The first step to getting what you want
is to have the courage
to get rid of what you don't."
– Zig Ziglar*

KEY OF INTUITIVE INTENTION

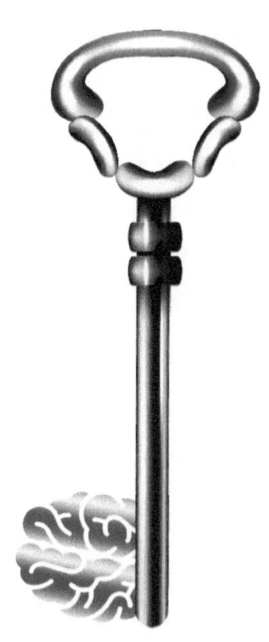

Unlock the gift of being the architect of your life. Empower yourself to make mindful choices that honor your well-being and authenticity, allowing you to live a passion-rich, purpose-driven life.

9

The Gift of Being the Architect of Your Life

Intuition is a powerful force that resides deep within each of us. It's an innate direct knowing and feeling that transcends the limitations of intellect. It bypasses the rational mind that goes straight to the heart. Intuition is often referred to as the sixth sense because it extends beyond the five physical senses. It is a powerful force of clarity that guides you in making choices and taking actions that are aligned with your highest potential. Your intuition provides you with insights and inner wisdom that may not be accessible through logical analysis alone as it surpasses rational thought.

Rooted deep within your subconscious, this subtle yet powerful guidance system that operates beyond conscious awareness, and is nudging you towards decisions, actions, and experiences is aligned with your deepest desires and values. Your intuition is shaped by your experiences, values, and beliefs. Your intuition often serves as a compass, guiding you toward the right path despite the obstacles and challenges you may face. Your intuition provides insights into the hidden patterns and connections with the world around you, allowing you to make informed choices and take proactive actions.

Learning to trust your intuition is an essential step in developing your intuitive abilities. It is not always easy to trust these subtle sensations and impulses, especially when faced with external pressures and expectations. By cultivating awareness of your intuition and following its guidance, you can begin to harness its power and enhance your life in a meaningful way.

Developing a regular practice of self-reflection and self-awareness can involve mirror work, meditation, journal writing, or any other practice that helps you connect with your inner self. By becoming more in tune with your thoughts, feelings, and sensations, you can start to recognize when your intuition is speaking to you.

Another crucial step in trusting your intuition is practicing discernment. This involves differentiating between intuition and mental noise or wishful thinking. Recognizing intuitive nudges involves being in a state of inner calm to distinguish genuine intuitive insights from the chatter of irrational fears, desires, or doubts that may cloud your judgment. Quieting the noise and distractions of daily life can make it easier to tune into your inner voice to gain clarity on your intentions.

When your intuition aligns with your core values and beliefs, it serves as a reliable guide and provides a sense of authenticity and conviction in your decisions and actions. Trusting your intuition under these circumstances empowers you to navigate life with greater confidence and alignment with your true self.

Keep in mind that it's important to let go of the need for immediate certainty and embrace the mystery and fluidity of life. Sometimes, your intuition may guide you towards paths that are not immediately apparent or logical. By trusting the process and being open to possibilities, you can allow yourself to make bold decisions that may lead to unexpected growth and fulfillment. Intuition is a powerful force that lies within all of us. By understanding its role and developing your ability to trust it, you can unlock a treasure trove of wisdom and guidance. Trusting your intuition can lead to a more fulfilling, authentic, and empowered life.

Align Intentions with Your Intuition

Intention is the conscious decision or purpose behind actions, while intuition is the inner knowing that guides you toward your most aligned path. When you set an intention without tapping into your intuition, you are operating solely from a rational mind by relying on logic, planning, and willpower to drive your actions. While this approach can be effective in achieving certain goals, it often overlooks the deeper wisdom and insights that intuition offers.

Without tapping into your intuition, your intentions may lack depth and authenticity. You might set goals based on external pressures or societal expectations rather than your true desires and values. As a result, your actions may feel forced or disconnected from your authentic self, leading to a sense of dissatisfaction or emptiness even when you achieve your goals. Furthermore, without intuition, you may overlook subtle signs and opportunities that could lead you toward your intentions more effortlessly.

You may become rigid in your approach and unwilling to adapt. You may refuse to course-correct when faced with unexpected challenges or detours. In essence, intention without intuition can feel like trying to navigate through a foggy forest without a map while unsure of your direction and disconnected from your inner guidance. When you set intentions aligned with your intuition, you tap into a source of wisdom and guidance that can help you make choices that resonate with you at a much deeper level. It leads to a higher likelihood of success and happiness.

By integrating intuition into your intention-setting process, you infuse your goals with authenticity, passion, and purpose. You become more attuned to the subtle whispers of your soul, allowing you to navigate life with greater clarity, alignment, and fulfillment. Ultimately, intention that is fueled by intuition, becomes a powerful force for creating a life that reflects your deepest desires and aspirations.

Intuitive intention relies on your ability to pick up on subtle cues and patterns in your environment, often without fully understanding the reasoning behind your impulses. These can be the sudden urge to take a different route home by sensing you may get caught in traffic otherwise, an unexpected feeling to talk to a stranger that leads to a meaningful conversation, or an instinctive knowing of when to trust someone and when to walk away.

Your intuitive guidance emerges from a combination of factors, including past experiences, learned associations, and innate instincts. Your brain is constantly processing vast amounts of information, much of which you may not consciously perceive. Yet, this information contributes to your intuition, shaping your perceptions and influencing your decisions. Moreover, intuitive intention often arises in moments of clarity when the noise of your mind quiets down, allowing you to tap into your deeper wisdom.

While intuitive intention may seem mysterious at times, it serves a vital purpose in guiding you toward growth, connection, and fulfillment. By tuning into your intuition and honoring its guidance, you can navigate life with greater clarity, authenticity, and alignment with your true self.

Your hopes and dreams are the fuel that propels you forward. This represents your vision for the future, painting a picture of the life you long to create for yourself. Yet amidst the hustle and bustle of daily life or past childhood traumas, you can lose sight of your dreams and drift away from your authentic path.

When navigating the journey toward fulfilling your dreams through intuitive intention without external validation or support, it can be easy to succumb to self-doubt and insecurity. That makes it harder to trust in your abilities and intuition. You may find yourself questioning whether your dreams are achievable or if you're simply chasing a fantasy. The absence of belief from others can lead to feelings of isolation and loneliness. It can feel like you're navigating the journey alone, without anyone to share your struggles, triumphs, and aspirations. This lack of connection can dampen your spirits and make it harder to stay motivated and focused on your goals.

However, not having anyone believe in you can also be a powerful catalyst for self-discovery and resilience. In the absence of external validation, you're forced to cultivate a deeper sense of self-belief and inner strength. Self-reliance and self-discovery can lead to a profound sense of empowerment by realizing that you don't need external validation to pursue your dreams or live authentically. Your worth and potential are not dependent on the beliefs of others. Your worth and potential ultimately stem from your inherent value and capabilities.

In the face of doubt and skepticism from others, your unwavering belief in yourself becomes a testament to your resilience and determination. You forge your own path that is guided by the wisdom of your intuition and the conviction of your intentions. As you continue to trust in yourself and follow your authentic path, you may find that your dreams are not only achievable but exceed even your wildest expectations.

The simple act of gazing into a mirror and truly seeing yourself without judgment or criticism, can open the door to profound self-awareness and intuitive wisdom.

Mirror Work

Mirror work serves as the first step in developing a deeper relationship with your authentic self. There have been many times when I've felt disconnected not just from others, but from myself. Looking in the mirror, I seldom recognized the person looking back at me. However, there were two teachers who saw something in me. One was my first-grade teacher, who praised me for my art talent, and the other was my high school English teacher who recognized my writing talent.

Believing what these teachers saw in me were the seeds of belief that led me to a deeper understanding of myself. There are still times when I get knocked down and make mistakes, but there's one thing I know for sure: when I look in the mirror today, I see who I truly am and smile.

In the intimate setting of looking at yourself in the mirror, you can examine your thoughts, emotions, and beliefs without filters and confront limiting beliefs that no longer serve you. It creates the space to plant the seeds of self-love and self-trust that are essential qualities for manifesting your deepest intentions.

As you embark on your journey, mirror work can become a powerful ally to help you see yourself with kindness and curiosity. Through this practice, you can learn to let go of harsh self-judgment and embrace the unique light that shines within you. This heightened self-awareness not only strengthens your intuitive guidance but also enhances your capacity for self-acceptance and self-trust, which are the foundations for creating lasting transformation from the inside out.

Mirror work can help you cultivate the ability to see yourself through the eyes of your soul and recognize the light that shines within you. It's a powerful technique used to tap into your inner wisdom and live with intention. It involves looking at yourself in the mirror while affirming positive statements or engaging in self-reflection. By focusing on your reflection, you can connect with your subconscious mind and harness the power of your intuition to set intentions and manifest your desires.

Engaging in intuitive intention mirror work can be a transformative practice that harnesses the power of your intuition to set intentions and manifest your desires. It involves using the mirror as a tool for deep self-reflection to access deeper levels of understanding and self-awareness.

When practicing mirror work, you can use affirmations to reaffirm positive beliefs about yourself and your life. Here are 10 affirmations to use for mirror work to help tap into your intuition. When using these affirmations during mirror work, look into your eyes and speak words with intention and conviction. Allow the affirmations to sink in and resonate within you, reinforcing your trust and connection with your intuitive self.

1. I am open and receptive to my inner wisdom and intuitive guidance.
2. I trust the messages and insights that come through my intuition.
3. My intuition is a powerful gift that helps me navigate life with clarity and purpose.
4. I release all doubts and embrace the truth of my intuitive knowing.
5. I am attuned to the subtle whispers of my soul and inner voice.
6. My intuition is a direct connection to the universal intelligence within me.
7. I honor my intuitive abilities and allow them to shine brightly.
8. I am confident in my ability to tune into my intuition and make empowered choices.
9. My intuition is a guiding light that illuminates my authentic path.
10. I am grateful for the intuitive wisdom that resides within me, and I commit to nurturing this sacred gift.

By repeating these affirmations while looking into your own eyes in the mirror, you reinforce these positive messages and shift your mindset toward one of self-love, confidence, and empowerment. Additionally, mirror work allows you to confront any negative thoughts or beliefs that may be holding you back. By facing yourself in the mirror, you are forced to confront these inner demons and challenge them head-on. This process can be uncomfortable at first, as it was for me, but it can ultimately lead to profound personal growth and transformation

Taking Mirror Work to the Next Level

When practicing intuitive intention mirror work, you begin by gazing into your own eyes in the mirror. This direct eye contact serves as a gateway to your subconscious, allowing you to access intuitive insights and guidance. As you look into the mirror, focus on setting intentions for what you want to manifest in your life, whether it be love, abundance, success, or personal growth.

As you affirm your intentions, pay attention to any intuitive nudges or feelings that arise within you. These intuitive insights can provide valuable guidance on the steps you need to take to align with your intentions and manifest your desires. Trusting your intuition in this process allows you to bypass the limitations of your logical mind and tap into a deeper knowing that resides within you.

Through regular practice of intuitive intention mirror work, you can strengthen your connection to your intuition, and gain clarity on your values, goals, and desires, allowing you to live in alignment with your true self and create the life you envision. You become more attuned to its guidance in all areas of your life. This heightened sense of intuition empowers you to make decisions that are in alignment with your highest good and navigate life with greater clarity and purpose.

Living with intention involves being mindful and purposeful in your actions, thoughts, and choices. Mirror work can help you align with your intentions by providing a space for reflection and introspection. Overall, mirror work is a valuable tool for cultivating self-awareness, building self-esteem, and living with intention. By incorporating this practice into your daily routine, you can tap into your inner wisdom, break free from limiting beliefs, unlock the unlimited potential that lies within you, and create a life filled with purpose, abundance, joy, and fulfillment.

Self Reflection Exercise

Here's a guide on how to effectively practice mirror work to tap into your inner wisdom and manifest your desires:

1. **Find a quiet and comfortable space:** Choose a quiet and comfortable space where you won't be disturbed. Make sure the lighting is soft and gentle to create a calming atmosphere.

2. **Set your intention:** Begin by setting a clear intention for your mirror work session. Think about what you want to manifest

in your life, whether it's love, abundance, success, or personal growth. Write down your intention to focus your energy and attention on it.

3. **Sit in front of a mirror:** Sit comfortably in front of a mirror with your back straight and shoulders relaxed. Gaze into your own eyes in the mirror, allowing yourself to make direct eye contact with your reflection.

4. **Take a few deep breaths:** Take a few deep breaths to center yourself and calm your mind. Allow yourself to relax and let go of any tension or stress you may be feeling.

5. **Affirm your intentions:** Begin affirming your intentions out loud or silently in your mind. Speak your intentions with confidence and conviction, visualizing them as already manifesting in your life. For example, you could say, "I am worthy of love and abundance," or "I am successful and fulfilled in all areas of my life."

6. **Pay attention to your intuition**: As you affirm your intentions, pay attention to any intuitive nudges or feelings that arise within you. Notice any insights or guidance that come to you during the process. Trust your intuition and allow it to guide you in setting intentions aligned with your highest good.

7. **Reflect and journal:** After completing your mirror work session, take some time to reflect on your experience. Journal any insights, feelings, or intuitive guidance you received during the practice. Reflect on how you can incorporate these insights into your daily life to manifest your desires.

8. **Practice regularly:** Intuitive intention mirror work is most effective when practiced regularly. Incorporate this practice into your daily or weekly routine to strengthen your connection to your intuition and manifest your desires more effectively.

By following these steps and incorporating mirror work into your routine, you can tap into your inner wisdom, set powerful intentions, and manifest the life of your dreams. Trust your intuition, listen closely, and embrace the endless possibilities that await you. Intuitive intuition can serve as a gateway to a deeper spiritual connection to the universal wisdom and divine intelligence that resides within us all.

Intuitive Intention Actions & Activities

Intuitive intentions are conscious choices and commitments you make to yourself that are guided by your inner truth and higher wisdom. They serve as a catalyst for positive change, helping you navigate life's challenges with clarity and purpose. By setting intuitive intentions, you create a roadmap for your personal evolution, one that honors your deepest desires and propels you toward a more fulfilling and meaningful existence.

Just as a seed requires nurturing to blossom into a vibrant flower, your intuitive intentions must be tended to with care and dedication. Engaging in regular practices that foster self-awareness can help you stay attuned to your inner voice and keep your intentions aligned with your authentic path.

Intuitive intention is a powerful practice that can bring about transformative changes in various aspects of our lives. By harnessing your intuition and setting clear intentions, you can manifest your dreams, overcome challenges, and create the life you desire. Start by reflecting on your core values, passions, and goals.

Self Reflection Exercise

Ask yourself:

- What do I truly long for?

- What brings me joy and fulfillment?

Once you have a sense of your intentions, write them down. Writing them down helps anchor them in reality and provides a physical reminder of the intentions you are setting. It also serves as a way to check in with yourself and ensure that your actions align with your intuitive intentions.

The next step is to get specific about what we want by visualizing them as if they have already manifested. It's important to let go of any limiting beliefs or doubts that may stand in the way of seeing yourself achieving what you want.

Intentions act as powerful magnets, drawing in opportunities and experiences that align with your desires. Taking inspired action is crucial in manifesting your desires. You must be willing to step out of your comfort zone and take action that will bring you closer to your goals. This may involve taking steps such as making lifestyle changes, pursuing education or training, or seeking out new experiences that align with your intentions.

Trusting your intuition and following your gut instincts can often lead to serendipitous encounters and opportunities that are in alignment with your desires. Maintaining a positive mindset is also essential for manifesting what you want in life. Negativity and doubt can block the flow of energy, preventing you from attracting what you desire. It's important to cultivate a mindset of abundance, gratitude, and belief in your ability to manifest your desires.

By identifying and understanding your heart's desires, setting clear intentions, taking inspired action, and maintaining a positive mindset, you can create a life that is aligned with your passions and dreams.

Trust in your intuition, follow your heart, and watch your desires unfold before your eyes.

Crafting a Vision Board

Another powerful tool for manifesting your dreams and goals is to create a vision board. A vision board is a visual representation of your desires. It's a fun and creative process that can help clarify your aspirations and keep you focused on achieving them. It consists of a compilation of images, words, and objects that represent the things you want to achieve or experience in life. By creating a vision board and placing it in a visible place, you can constantly be reminded of your goals and stay motivated to work towards them.

Benefits of a Vision Board

- **Clarifies Goals:** When you create a vision board, you clarify what you really want. By visualizing your goals, you're more likely to stay focused on achieving them.
- **Motivation:** Having a visual representation of your goals can serve as a constant reminder of what you're working towards. This can help boost motivation during challenging times.
- **Visualization:** Visualization is a powerful technique used by athletes, performers, and successful individuals to achieve their goals. A vision board serves as a tool for visualizing your ideal future, making it seem more achievable.
- **Inspiration:** Surrounding yourself with images and words that inspire you can help you generate new ideas and possibilities. This vision board can spark creativity and innovation.
- **Focus:** With so many distractions in today's world, it's easy to lose focus on what truly matters. A vision board keeps your goals front and center, helping you prioritize your time and energy.

Materials Needed

To craft an effective vision board, we will need to gather some materials.

Here is a list of materials you will need:

- A large piece of cardboard or poster board
- Scissors
- Glue or double-sided tape
- Magazines, newspapers, or other sources of images
- Pens or markers
- Inspirational quotes or mantras
- Pictures of your goals or dreams
- Decorative items such as stickers, washi tape, or glitter

Directions

Crafting a vision board is a simple and straightforward process. By following these simple steps, you can create a vision board that serves as a visual representation of your goals and aspirations. Remember, a vision board is a reflection of what you want to create for yourself, so take your time to make it personal and meaningful.

1. Find a quiet and comfortable space to work on your vision board. This can be a dedicated area in your home or even a quiet corner in your workplace.

2. Gather all the materials you need. Place the cardboard or poster board in front of you. Have your scissors, glue, magazines, pens, and any additional decorative items.

3. Start by gathering images of your goals or dreams. These can be photos, magazine cutouts, or even drawings. Look for images that evoke feelings of joy, motivation, and inspiration.

4. Once you have collected your images, lay them out on the cardboard or poster board in an arrangement that appeals to you. Try to create a visually pleasing and balanced composition.

5. Once you have arranged the images, start writing down any positive affirmations or mantras that resonate with you. These can help remind you of your values and aspirations.

6. Add some personal touches to your vision board. This can include incorporating objects that represent your goals, such as travel tickets, concert tickets, or postcards from places you want to visit.

7. Finally, glue or tape down all the images and affirmations onto the board. Make sure it is securely attached and placed in an area where you will see it often.

Take some time to regularly reflect on your vision board and visualize your goals and dreams. Keep in mind that nothing is set in stone. You can modify and make any changes you wish to make to your vision board. You can also create several different vision boards, each for a specific purpose.

The whole idea of creating a vision board is to have a visual reminder of what you are working towards. Your vision board(s) can help keep you motivated and inspired on your journey toward achieving the life you want.

Speaking of motivations, as you continue to work toward manifesting your desires, it's important to pause and examine the underlying motivations behind them. Ask yourself:

- Are these aspirations truly aligned with my authentic self and deepest values, or are they being fueled by external pressures, societal expectations, or ego-driven desires for validation or status?

The journey of personal growth and self-discovery requires that you be willing to peel back the layers and discern between the fleeting wants of the ego and the enduring callings of the soul. In the next couple of chapters, we'll explore how to differentiate between ego-driven desires and soul-aligned intentions. We'll then delve into some mindfulness practices.

"The more you are in touch with your intention, the more your life flows and aligns with your purpose."
– Oprah Winfrey

10

The Nature of the Ego and the Soul

Discerning between ego-driven desires and soul-aligned intentions involves navigating the complexities of your motivations, desires, and aspirations to distinguish between superficial wants driven by your ego and deeper, authentic intentions that resonate with your true essence and purpose. This process of discernment requires self-awareness, introspection, and a willingness to delve beneath the surface of your desires.

Ego vs. Soul

The ego represents your sense of self-identity shaped by external influences such as societal norms, past experiences, and conditioned beliefs. The ego craves validation, control, and security, often seeking immediate gratification and external recognition. Ego-driven desires are often fueled by fear, comparison, and the need to conform to societal expectations, which can often leave you feeling empty or unfulfilled once you achieve something.

On the other hand, your soul embodies your authentic essence and connection to a higher purpose or universal consciousness. Soul-aligned intentions stem from a place of inner wisdom, unconditional love, and alignment with your deepest values and aspirations. These intentions resonate with your inner truth and contribute to your spiritual growth, fulfillment, and sense of meaning. To discern between ego-driven desires and soul-aligned intentions, consider the following:

- **Ego-driven desires** are often rooted in external validation, fear of failure, or comparison to others.
- **Soul-aligned intentions** arise from a sense of inner calling, alignment with core values, and a desire for genuine growth and contribution.

- **Ego-driven desires** tend to provide temporary satisfaction but lack lasting fulfillment.
- **Soul-aligned intentions** cultivate deep and sustainable fulfillment, that aligns with your purpose and authentic self.

- **Ego-driven desires** may be clouded by doubts, insecurities, and superficial needs.
- **Soul-aligned intentions** are characterized by clarity, alignment with your inner truth, and a sense of inner peace.

- **Ego-driven desires** may prioritize your individual gain or validation at the expense of others.
- **Soul-aligned intentions** consider the greater good and seek to uplift and inspire both yourself and others.

- **Ego-driven desires** may conflict with your core values or lead to compromises that undermine your integrity.
- **Soul-aligned intentions** are congruent with your values and contribute to your personal growth and authenticity.

Aligning Core Values with Integrity

Living a fulfilling and purpose-driven life begins with a deep understanding of your core values and a commitment to uphold them with unwavering integrity. Core values represent the essence of who you are and what you cherish most in life. Your core values serve as guiding principles that shape your decisions, actions, and relationships.

Your core values are the fundamental beliefs and principles that define your identity and guide your choices. They are deeply rooted in your personal experiences, upbringing, and worldview. Common core values include authenticity, compassion, honesty, resilience, family, creativity, justice, and many others. Identifying your core values requires introspection and reflection on what matters most to you and what principles you want to embody in your life.

Living with integrity involves aligning your core values with your actions. Living in alignment with your core values and integrity is demonstrated through your honesty, reliability, conduct, accountability, and respect for yourself and others, even in the face of challenges or temptations. Upholding your integrity during challenges builds resilience and inner strength. This empowers you to navigate life's difficulties with grace. Integrity builds trust, credibility, and authenticity in your relationships and interactions. Integrity fosters respect and forms the foundation for healthy and meaningful connections with others.

Core values serve as a compass that guides you in making ethical and meaningful decisions aligned with your principles and beliefs. Aligning your actions with your core values leads to a sense of purpose, satisfaction, and inner harmony. It cultivates a deep sense of fulfillment and contentment. Embracing them and upholding integrity in all aspects of your life, empowers you to lead with integrity, make a positive impact, and cultivate a sense of fulfillment and inner peace.

Take time to identify your core values through introspection and self-discovery. Reflect on what truly matters to you and what principles you want to embody. Actively align your actions and decisions with your core values in daily life by making conscious choices that honor them and contribute to your sense of authenticity. Regularly revisit and refine your core values based on life experiences and personal growth. Allow yourself to evolve and adapt while staying true to your authentic self.

Misaligned Actions: Addressing the Disconnect

But what happens when your actions are out of wack with your values? First of all, realize that we are all human and make mistakes. Be compassionate with yourself and use setbacks as opportunities for growth and learning. Living in conflict with your core values can hinder your personal growth and ability to lead a fulfilling life.

Take for instance anger. When you experience anger or frustration, especially in challenging situations, it can cloud your judgment and override your usual values-based decision-making. These strong emotions can trigger impulsive reactions or defensive behaviors that may contradict your core values. For example, when feeling angry, you might lash out verbally or resort to aggression, even if you value kindness and empathy. The intensity of anger and frustration can also lead you to prioritize short-term relief over long-term values. In moments of heightened emotion, you may seek immediate gratification or seek to alleviate discomfort, disregarding the potential consequences to your values and relationships.

Addressing anger and frustrations requires self-awareness and emotional regulation. By recognizing the triggers that evoke these emotions, you can develop healthier coping mechanisms and strategies to respond in ways that align with your values. This involves cultivating mindfulness, pausing before reacting, practicing empathy, and developing communication skills to express your emotions constructively without compromising your values. By cultivating emotional awareness and resilience, you can navigate challenging situations with integrity and authenticity, even in the face of strong emotions.

Not being true to your values can erode trust in your relationships as others will perceive you as inconsistent, inauthentic, or unreliable, which leads to strained connections and misunderstandings. Imagine a scenario where your core value is honesty, but you find yourself in a situation where you feel compelled to lie or deceive others to avoid consequences or gain approval. This conflict between honesty and dishonesty creates a sense of inner turmoil. You might experience feelings of guilt, shame, or self-doubt as your actions contradict your deeply held beliefs.

Similarly, if one of your core values is compassion, yet you consistently find yourself acting in ways that are unkind or indifferent toward others, you may experience a disconnection within yourself. This inner conflict can manifest as anxiety or make you feel out of alignment with your true self. Addressing this inner conflict and realigning with your values is essential for personal growth, emotional well-being, and living authentically. By acknowledging and addressing this conflict, you create an opportunity for self-reflection and growth.

Allow yourself to explore the underlying reasons behind your actions. Identify areas where your behavior may not be in alignment with your true beliefs and principles. Realize that your values can change. Realigning them can be a transformative journey that involves self-discovery and self-acceptance. It requires you to be willing to confront uncomfortable truths about yourself to gain clarity on what truly matters to you and what values you want to embody in your life. This process fosters self-awareness and authenticity, enabling you to make intentional choices aligned with your aspirations.

Addressing inner conflict promotes emotional healing and resilience. It allows you to heal wounds from past experiences and let go of limiting beliefs or negative patterns that no longer serve you. When you embrace your values and live with integrity, you cultivate a greater sense of inner peace and fulfillment. You empower yourself to navigate life's challenges with grace and confidence, knowing that your actions are guided by principles that reflect your true essence.

By embracing your authenticity, you strengthen your emotional resilience and cultivate meaningful connections with others. Honoring your values and living with integrity creates a life filled with purpose, fulfillment, and genuine happiness. However, to truly embody these principles and live from a place of alignment, it's essential to cultivate self-awareness and presence. One powerful way to achieve this is through mindfulness and meditation practices.

Mindfulness and Meditation

Imagine you're sitting quietly, taking a moment to just be present. You might start noticing your breath and how it feels as you inhale and exhale. As you do this, perhaps thoughts may pop into your mind or sensations might arise in your body. With mindfulness, you acknowledge these thoughts and sensations without judgment. For example, if you notice feelings of anxiety or stress, you don't criticize yourself for feeling that way. Instead, you observe these feelings with curiosity and acceptance.

Mindfulness

Mindfulness is about becoming more aware of your inner world, such as your thoughts, emotions, and bodily sensations, as well as the external world around you. By practicing mindfulness regularly, you develop a greater capacity to stay centered and calm, even during challenging situations. This heightened awareness can help you respond more thoughtfully to stressors rather than have you react impulsively based on automatic habits or emotions.

One of the beautiful things about mindfulness is its versatility. It can be practiced formally through meditation sessions, where you dedicate specific time to sit and focus on your breath or body sensations. It can also be integrated into everyday activities. For instance, while eating, you might pay attention to the flavors, textures, and sensations of each bite, savoring the experience fully. During a walk, you might also notice the sights, sounds, and smells around you, grounding yourself in the present moment.

Over time, the benefits of mindfulness can become quite profound. Research has shown that regular mindfulness can reduce symptoms of anxiety and depression, enhance focus and attention, and even strengthen the immune system. Moreover, mindfulness fosters a sense of inner peace and resilience that extends beyond formal practice sessions, which enriches your overall quality of life. The key is to approach mindfulness with an open mind and gentle curiosity, allowing yourself to explore your inner landscape without expectation or judgment. It's a journey of self-discovery and self-compassion that can lead to profound insights and a deeper connection with yourself and the world around you.

Dealing with a Wandering Mind

A common experience during mindfulness or meditation practice is the mind's tendency to wander. Thoughts, memories, and concerns often arise, pulling attention away from the present moment. The key to managing a wandering mind is to approach it with kindness and non-judgment. Instead of getting frustrated or critical, gently guide your awareness back to your chosen anchor like your breath or body sensations. Recognize that it's normal for the mind to wander. Each moment of awareness is an opportunity to practice coming back to the present. Over time, with patience and persistence, you'll develop greater focus and stability.

Managing Discomfort and Resistance

Mindfulness can bring up discomfort, both physical and emotional. When faced with discomfort or resistance it's essential to approach these experiences with openness and curiosity. Rather than trying to push away or suppress discomfort, acknowledge it with compassion. Explore the sensations or emotions mindfully. Observe them without attaching judgments or narratives. By cultivating a willingness to be present with discomfort, you can develop greater resilience and acceptance. Sometimes, adjusting your posture or taking gentle steps to care for yourself can also alleviate physical discomfort, allowing you to continue more comfortably.

Navigating Distractions

External distractions, such as noises or interruptions, as well as internal distractions like racing thoughts or emotions, can be challenging. The key is not to eliminate distractions, it's to learn to relate to them differently. Start by acknowledging the distraction without getting caught up in it. Notice the distraction as it arises. Then gently guide your attention back to your focal point. Use distractions as opportunities to practice refocusing and cultivating greater awareness. Sometimes, incorporating distractions into your practice by simply noticing them can deepen your mindfulness skills. Additionally, creating a conducive environment for practice; whether it's finding a quiet space or using headphones to minimize external noises can support your ability to stay present despite distractions.

Living Mindfully

Living mindfully means embracing the present moment fully and consciously, without being preoccupied with the past or future. When you live mindfully, you engage with life as it unfolds in the here and now, allowing yourself to reawaken to the richness of each moment. This practice involves letting go of regrets, resentments, or nostalgia associated with the past,. This includes releasing anxieties, worries, or fantasies about the future.

Living mindfully involves recognizing that the present moment is the only moment that truly exists. It's about paying attention to your immediate experience along with your thoughts, feelings, sensations, and surroundings without judgment or attachment. By anchoring yourself in the present, you become more attuned to the beauty and intricacy of the life unfolding around you.

Mindful living is not about ignoring responsibilities or avoiding planning altogether; rather, it's about approaching these aspects of life with clarity and presence. When you focus on the present moment, you bring a sense of intentionality and awareness to your actions and decisions. This leads to greater fulfillment, as you savor the simple joys of life that often go unnoticed when the mind is preoccupied with the past or future.

Living mindfully can also cultivate a deeper sense of gratitude and connection. By tuning into the present moment, you may discover a newfound appreciation for the people in your life, the beauty of nature, or the sensations of everyday experiences. This heightened awareness fosters a sense of liveliness and authenticity, allowing you to respond to life's challenges and joys with greater resilience and compassion.

Ultimately, living mindfully means embracing the gift of each moment. It's recognizing that life unfolds in the present and that true happiness and peace can be found by fully inhabiting the here and now. Mindfulness invites you to let go of distractions and immerse yourself in the reality of your experience moment by moment while awakening to the infinite possibilities and wonders that exist.

Meditation

There are many different styles and methods for meditation, some more structured than others. Meditation-focused practices can involve repeating mantras, guided visualizations, sound therapy, movement, and the use of other techniques to train the mind. Often these focused techniques and training are designed to achieve specific mental, emotional, or spiritual goals that lead to profound changes in cognition, emotion regulation, spiritual enlightenment, and well-being.

In any case, meditation can be very simple and effective. To get started, spend a few minutes doing breathwork to center yourself. Inhale slowly through your nose and allow your belly to expand. Pause briefly, and then exhale through pursed lips. Repeat this cyclical breathing until you feel grounded in the present moment. From this relaxed state, turn your attention inward. Instead of forcing intention statements (affirmation), what you want to do is open yourself up to receiving inner messages. Your goal is to find desires and goals bubbling up organically from your subconscious mind. Be open and curious by simply witnessing whatever arises without judgment.

The intentions born from meditation arise from the depths of your being. They are aligned with your authentic self, increasing their potency for manifestation. Integrate these intuitive intentions into your vision board, rituals, and daily life. Revisit them frequently through meditation to renew their energy and anchor them into your consciousness.

Meditation forms the channel for you to tune into the intuitive guidance within. It is a quiet space where you can hear the whispers of your soul's truth and align your intentions accordingly. Let meditation be the bridge illuminating your path of conscious creation and soul-led manifestation.

Sometimes, despite your best intentions, you may still encounter internal resistance that can manifest as self-sabotaging behaviors that would hinder your ability to live congruently with your values and achieve your aspirations.

Self-sabotage can take many forms, from procrastination and self-doubt to self-destructive habits and toxic relationships. In the next chapter, we'll explore these self-sabotaging behaviors in-depth, shedding light on their underlying causes and equipping you with more strategies to overcome them.

11

Self-Sabotaging Behaviors

Self-sabotaging behaviors are patterns of negative actions that you may engage in that hinder your progress, goals, and overall happiness. These behaviors often stem from underlying issues or beliefs that you may have about yourself or the world around you.

Some common self-sabotaging behaviors include negative self-talk, where you constantly criticize yourself and question your abilities, which leads to feelings of inadequacy and self-doubt. Isolating yourself to avoid social interactions or difficult conversations can also be a form of self-sabotage driven by social anxiety or discomfort. Remaining in toxic relationships characterized by conflict, criticism, or emotional abuse can also be self-sabotage as it perpetuates feelings of unworthiness or fears of being alone.

Engaging in negative habits such as excessive drinking, overeating, or addictive behaviors may serve as a way to cope with emotional pain through self-punishment. This pattern is driven by deep-seated feelings of inadequacy or unworthiness, where you anticipate failure and resort to self-destructive actions to validate your negative self-perceptions. Some individuals exhibit self-sabotage through narcissistic tendencies or self-destruction. They seek attention or experience emotional pain as a means of reinforcing negative beliefs about themselves.

Another aspect of self-sabotage involves setting yourself up to fail or maintaining a cycle of failure to reinforce your beliefs of inadequacy. This behavior is often rooted in fears of failure or a lack of self-confidence. By sabotaging opportunities or underperforming deliberately, you perpetuate a negative narrative. This then confirms your belief that you are not capable or deserving of success.

Self-sabotaging behaviors can manifest in various aspects of life, including relationships, careers, health, and personal development. One of the defining characteristics of self-sabotage is the internal conflict it creates within you. Often, the underlying psychological factors at play are fear of failure, low self-esteem, perfectionism, or a deep-seated belief that you are unworthy of success and happiness. Understanding these factors requires delving into the intricate interplay of your personal experiences, upbringing, societal influences, and the internal thought patterns that have shaped your self-concept and behavior.

Understanding Fear of Failure

Fear of failure is an intense emotion that plays a pivotal role in self-sabotaging behavior by creating self-imposed barriers and limiting beliefs that hinder your personal development and negatively affect your drive for achievement. You fear not meeting expectations or disappointing yourself and others. You fear negative consequences for your perceived inadequacies. This fear often develops from early childhood experiences, societal pressures, or past traumatic events.

For instance, a child who faces consistent criticism or punishment for making mistakes may internalize the belief that failure is unacceptable and that they are inadequate. As they grow older, this belief can evolve into a pervasive fear of failure that shapes their behavior and decision-making processes.

Fear of failure manifests in various behaviors and thought patterns that ultimately hinder personal growth and success. Procrastination is a common response to this fear. You may delay important tasks to avoid the anxiety and discomfort associated with potential failure. Similarly, perfectionism often arises from the fear of not meeting high standards or expectations. This leads you to excessively critique your work, set unrealistic goals, or avoid taking risks altogether. Self-doubt also thrives in the presence of fear of failure. This erodes self-confidence and causes you to second-guess your abilities or downplay your achievements.

When you fear failure, you may subconsciously avoid challenging tasks or opportunities that hold potential for your growth and success. This avoidance behavior perpetuates a cycle of stagnation and missed opportunities. Your fear of failure can become a self-fulfilling prophecy, where you sabotage your efforts to align your negative beliefs about yourself. This might involve underperforming deliberately or disengaging from activities that could lead to your success.

Overcoming your fear of failure is a transformative journey that involves cultivating resilience, reframing your negative beliefs, and developing a healthier relationship with success and setbacks. By identifying, challenging, and replacing your underlying beliefs about failure and self-worth and recognizing distorted thinking patterns, you can begin to adopt more realistic and compassionate perspectives.

Building resilience is essential in embracing setbacks as valuable learning experiences rather than indicators of personal failure. Setting attainable goals and focusing on progress rather than perfection fosters a growth-oriented mindset and encourages continuous improvement.

By acknowledging and addressing your fear of failure, you can liberate yourself from self-sabotaging behaviors and embrace a mindset that values growth, resilience, and self-compassion. Through intentional self-awareness and proactive steps toward personal development, you can navigate challenges with confidence and authenticity. This ultimately unlocks your full potential and allows you to pursue fulfilling paths in life.

Understanding Low Self-Esteem

Low self-esteem is a persistent feeling of inadequacy, self-doubt, or worthlessness that undermines your sense of self-worth and overall well-being. With low self-esteem, you may harbor negative beliefs about yourself and your abilities. You may view yourself in a critical and unfavorable light. This negative self-perception can stem from early childhood experiences, societal influences, or traumatic events that shaped your self-concept and interpersonal relationships.

The origins of low self-esteem can be complex and multifaceted. If as a child you experienced neglect, rejection, or abuse during critical developmental stages you may have internalized negative messages about your worth and capabilities. Similarly, growing up in environments where achievement and appearance are prioritized over intrinsic qualities can contribute to feelings of inadequacy and self-doubt. Traumatic events such as bullying, loss, or failure can also significantly impact self-esteem and contribute to self-sabotaging behaviors later in life.

Low self-esteem manifests in various behaviors and thought patterns that perpetuate self-sabotage and hinder personal growth. With low self-esteem, you may engage in excessive self-criticism by constantly doubting your abilities and diminishing your accomplishments. You may avoid taking risks or pursuing opportunities for fear of failure or rejection, limiting your growth potential.

Additionally, low self-esteem can contribute to unhealthy coping mechanisms such as substance abuse, overeating, or self-isolation as a means of numbing emotional pain or avoiding confrontations with your perceived shortcomings.

Low self-esteem significantly contributes to self-sabotage by reinforcing negative beliefs and behaviors that undermine personal development and well-being. With low self-esteem, you may engage in self-sabotaging behaviors as a way to validate your negative self-perceptions or avoid situations that challenge your fragile self-image. This can manifest as missing opportunities for advancement, self-sabotaging relationships, or settling for less than you deserve due to feelings of unworthiness.

Addressing low self-esteem is essential for breaking free from self-sabotaging patterns to foster self-acceptance and personal growth. By exploring the origins of self-doubt and developing healthier beliefs about yourself, you can cultivate self-compassion and self-acceptance. Building resilience through positive affirmations, self-care practices, and supportive relationships can also empower you to navigate challenges with confidence and authenticity.

Addressing low self-esteem involves recognizing its origins, manifestations, and impact on your self-sabotaging behaviors. Through intentional self-reflection and compassionate self-care, you can overcome feelings of inadequacy, embrace your inherent worth, and pursue meaningful paths toward self-fulfillment and well-being.

Understanding Perfectionism

Perfectionism is a personality trait characterized by setting exceedingly high standards for yourself and being excessively critical of your perceived failures or imperfections. It often stems from a deep-seated need for validation, acceptance, or control. Perfectionists tend to equate their self-worth with their achievements and may engage in rigid, all-or-nothing thinking patterns. While striving for excellence can be positive, perfectionism becomes detrimental when you become fixated on flawless performance and are unable to tolerate any form of perceived failure or mistake.

The origins of perfectionism can be rooted in childhood experiences, societal influences, or past traumas. If as a child you received conditional love or approval based solely on your achievements you may have internalized the belief that your worth is contingent upon meeting exceptionally high standards. Similarly, growing up in environments that emphasize competition and comparison can reinforce perfectionistic behaviors as you seek validation and acceptance through your accomplishments.

Perfectionism manifests in various behaviors and thought patterns that contribute to self-sabotage and hinder personal growth. Perfectionists are often hypercritical of themselves, magnifying even minor flaws or mistakes that would then erode self-confidence and lead to chronic feelings of inadequacy. You may set unattainably high standards for yourself, leading to chronic stress and burnout. Fear of not meeting your lofty standards can cause you to avoid challenges or new experiences, limiting your opportunities for growth and personal development.

Perfectionism contributes significantly to self-sabotage by creating a cycle of unattainable expectations and fear of failure. As a perfectionist you may procrastinate on tasks because you fear not being able to complete them perfectly, resulting in missed deadlines and increased stress. You may often be overly concerned with how others perceive you, leading to avoidance of opportunities for fear of judgment or criticism.

Additionally, perfectionists struggle to bounce back from setbacks or criticism, viewing any deviation from perfection as a personal failure. This hinders progress and perpetuates self-sabotaging behaviors.

Overcoming perfectionism requires self-awareness, self-compassion, and a willingness to challenge perfectionistic beliefs and behaviors. By cultivating a more balanced and compassionate perspective on achievement and self-worth, you can set realistic and achievable goals. You can celebrate progress rather than fixate on unattainable ideals.

Practicing self-compassion involves treating yourself with kindness and understanding, especially in moments of perceived failure or setback. This helps develop resilience and encourages you to embrace imperfection as a natural part of the human experience. Addressing perfectionism is essential for breaking free from self-sabotaging behaviors and fostering personal growth and fulfillment.

Through intentional self-reflection, therapy, and the cultivation of a growth-oriented mindset, you can harness your potential, navigate challenges with resilience, and pursue goals authentically and confidently.

Understanding Deep-Seated Belief of Unworthiness

A deep-seated belief of unworthiness is a pervasive and ingrained sense of being fundamentally flawed, and undeserving of success, happiness, or meaningful relationships. This belief often originates from early experiences of rejection, neglect, or trauma that shaped your self-concept and interpersonal relationships. With a deep-seated belief of unworthiness, you internalize negative messages about your value and worthiness, leading to persistent feelings of inadequacy and self-doubt.

The origins of this deep-seated belief can be traced back to childhood experiences, familial dynamics, or societal influences that reinforce feelings of inadequacy. If as a child you experienced consistent rejection, criticism, or abandonment you may have internalized the belief that you are inherently unlovable or unworthy of acceptance. Similarly, growing up in environments where self-worth is tied to external validation or unrealistic standards can contribute to feelings of unworthiness and self-sabotaging behaviors later in life.

A deep-seated belief of unworthiness manifests in various behaviors and thought patterns that perpetuate self-sabotage and hinder personal growth. With this belief, you may engage in self-sabotaging behaviors as a way to reaffirm your negative self-perception or avoid situations that challenge your core beliefs. This can include sabotaging relationships by pushing away supportive partners, settling for less than you deserve in various areas of life, or engaging in self-destructive habits as a means of coping with emotional pain.

A deep-seated belief in unworthiness significantly contributes to self-sabotage by reinforcing negative self-perceptions and maladaptive coping strategies. With this belief, you may sabotage opportunities for success or happiness because you feel undeserving or fear being exposed as inadequate. This can lead to missed chances for personal growth, fulfillment, and meaningful connections with others.

Additionally, feelings of unworthiness can perpetuate cycles of self-criticism, self-doubt, and self-sabotage that undermine overall well-being and life satisfaction. Addressing this feeling is essential for breaking free from self-sabotaging patterns and fostering self-acceptance and personal growth. By exploring the origins of unworthiness and developing healthier perspectives you can cultivate self-compassion, self-acceptance, and resilience.

Overcoming Self-Sabotage

Addressing a deep-seated belief of unworthiness involves recognizing its origins, manifestations, and impact on your self-sabotaging behaviors. Through intentional self-reflection and compassionate self-care, you can overcome feelings of inadequacy, embrace your inherent worth, and pursue meaningful paths toward self-fulfillment and authentic living.

Our family dynamics, particularly in dysfunctional environments, can profoundly shape our self-perception, relationships, and coping mechanisms. Unresolved childhood traumas, unhealthy communication patterns, or toxic family roles can perpetuate negative narratives that we internalize, leading to self-sabotage later in life. In the next chapter, we'll explore family dynamics how our environment contributes to self-limiting beliefs and behaviors, and how to break free from their grip.

KEY OF FAMILY AND FRIENDS

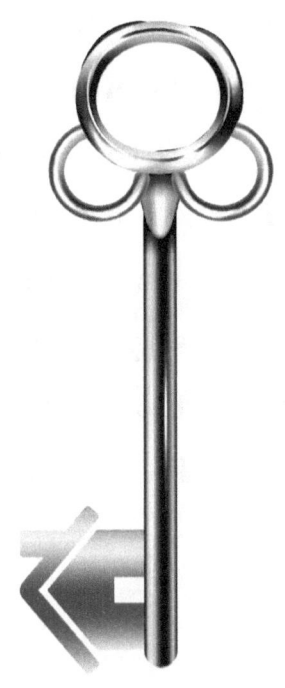

Unlock the gift of discovering the importance of connection and support in fostering emotional and spiritual growth. Meaningful connections with family and friends become essential pillars in your healing journey. Through these relationships, you learn the power of empathy and compassion that extends beyond yourself.

12

The Gift of Family, Friends, and You

Family and friends are integral parts of life. They influence who you are and significantly shape your personality. They can play significant roles, both positive and negative. As a child, you contribute to the family dynamic, bringing joy, love, and purpose. But you can also bring challenges and demands. Let's explore the roles your family, your friends, and you as the child play in shaping your life experience.

The Role of Family

Your family is foundational to your existence. They are the people who provide you with your first glimpse of love, support, and guidance. Their influence on you continues throughout your life.

On the positive side, family plays a crucial role in our upbringing. They provide a safe and nurturing home environment where we can feel protected. Their love and care help us develop a sense of self-worth and security. They teach us important values, beliefs, and traditions that form the core of our identities. Family is our origin, where we grow, and where we belong.

However, family relationships can be complex and multifaceted. They encompass both joyful and challenging experiences. Despite the challenges, family members are there for each other. They offer comfort, guidance, and a sense of belonging. The bonds created within families last a lifetime and are a source of strength during the happiest and most difficult times.

On the negative side, family influence can sometimes be detrimental. Families can sometimes be a source of conflict, stress, and negativity. Dysfunctional family dynamics can lead to emotional trauma, low self-esteem, and even mental health issues. Families may also have unrealistic expectations for their children, which leads to feelings of inadequacy and pressure.

The Role of Friends

Your friends are more than just acquaintances; they are companions who share laughter, adventures, and experiences with you on your life's journey. They provide camaraderie, support, and fun. Friends have a unique ability to know and understand us in a way that our family may not. They celebrate our victories and offer a listening ear during difficult times. They share our joys, sorrows, and everyday moments, creating an irreplaceable bond.

On the positive side, friends provide a much-needed escape valve from the stresses of daily life. Spending time with friends allows us to relax and recharge, fostering a sense of belonging and connection. They help us navigate the challenges of adolescence and adulthood, by offering valuable advice and perspective. Friends can enrich your life by expanding your horizons.

However, there can also be some negative effects on friendships. Peer pressure can have a strong influence on your choices and decisions. Friends who engage in negative behaviors, such as substance abuse or recklessness, can lead you astray. Friendships can also be a source of conflict and stress, especially if they do not align with your values or goals.

Your Role as a Child

As a child in your family, you play a pivotal role in shaping the dynamics and contributing to the overall family experience. On one hand, you bring immense joy, love, and purpose to your family. You provide a sense of renewal and hope, reminding your parents and loved ones of the beauty and wonder of life. Your laughter and innocence can lighten even the darkest of days, which brings your family together and creates cherished memories.

Moreover, you offer your family the opportunity to learn and grow. Through your curiosity and inquisitiveness, you challenge your parents and caregivers to be patient, understanding, and open-minded. Your child-like perspective can provide fresh insights and encourage your family to see the world through a different lens.

However, your role as a child also comes with challenges and potential negative aspects. Your need for attention, guidance, and care can be demanding, physically and emotionally for your parents and caregivers. Raising you can also be a significant financial burden that adds stress and strain to your family dynamics.

In some cases, you may face difficulties, such as learning disabilities, behavioral issues, or health problems that can place additional strain on your family. These challenges can test the resilience and coping mechanisms of both you and your loved ones.

Furthermore, your actions and behaviors can sometimes contribute to conflicts within your family unit. Sibling rivalries, defiance towards parental authority, or even unintentional misbehavior can create tension and disharmony within the household.

Despite these potential challenges, your role as the child remains central to the family dynamic. You bring a unique and invaluable perspective to your family that shapes the experiences and memories that bind your loved ones together for a lifetime. Just as you contribute to the family dynamic, you also play a vital role in shaping friendships as you bring joy, laughter, and a fresh outlook to those close to you.

The Impact of Family and Friends

The impact of family and friends can be profound and enduring. They are your primary agents of socialization during your childhood and adolescence. You learned behavioral norms, values, and attitudes by observing and imitating the behaviors of your family members and peers. For example, children often model their parents' communication styles, problem-solving approaches, and interpersonal skills.

Having a healthy relationship with your family and friends provides you with emotional support, validation, and nurturing,. These are essential for developing a secure sense of self and emotional resilience. These positive experiences of warmth, empathy, and affection within these relationships contribute to positive self-esteem and emotional well-being.

Interactions with family and friends can provide continuous feedback and validation for your behavior and identity. Constructive feedback and encouragement from loved ones can reinforce adaptive personality traits and behaviors, while criticism or neglect can contribute to self-doubt and insecurity. Your interactions with family members and friends can also enhance your social skills and communication abilities. Engaging in conversations, resolving conflicts, and navigating social dynamics within these relationships contribute to the development of interpersonal skills, assertiveness, and empathy.

Your family and friends most likely exposed you to diverse perspectives, beliefs, and experiences, which foster cognitive development and open-mindedness. Exposure to different viewpoints encourages critical thinking, empathy, and tolerance that shape your attitudes and personality traits.

Family and friends can also provide a social context for identity formation. As you interact with others, you develop a sense of belonging and identity within social groups. Supportive relationships contribute to a positive self-concept while conflicts or dysfunctional dynamics may lead to identity confusion or negative self-perceptions.

Family and friends influence lifestyle choices, habits, and behaviors. Shared activities, interests, and traditions within social networks contribute to the adoption of certain behaviors and values. These influence personality traits related to lifestyle preferences and social behaviors.

Overall, your family and friends serve as important social influences that shape your personality through socialization, emotional support, feedback, and interpersonal interactions. Positive relationships characterized by trust, empathy, and mutual respect foster healthy personality development. Meanwhile negative or dysfunctional relationships contribute to more maladaptive personality traits and emotional difficulties.

Recognizing the impact of these significant relationships allows you to make decisions to further cultivate supportive and nurturing relationships. These can promote personal growth, resilience, and well-being. Alternatively, relationships that do otherwise can be identified to determine whether it may be time to set some boundaries.

Personal Story: *Growing Up in a Dysfunctional Family*

Growing up, the effects of my father's alcoholism and my mother's struggles with obesity and codependency cast a shadow over my childhood, shaping my experiences and perceptions in profound ways.

My father, an auto mechanic, spent long hours at work and then retreated to local bars to unwind thereafter. On his days off from work, my father retreated to the backyard, where he could be found rolling cigarettes, or in the makeshift darkroom behind the garage developing rolls of black and white film he had taken with his 35mm camera. He was a quiet, meat-and-potatoes kind of guy, often eating dinner alone in the living room in front of the TV. This was a stark contrast to the vibrant Italian cuisine we indulged in at the dining room table.

Though I longed to be my father's little princess, my mother's efforts to shield my brother and me from our father's addiction by drilling into us, "Alcoholism is in your blood," may have been a blessing in disguise. Her words of warning such as "You can never drink" and "Stay away from your filthy father" although cutting, proved to be a guiding force in my life. It steered me away from the inclination to drink or date anyone who did.

My mother's insecurities about my father's addiction led us to live with her parents. Living with my grandparents was like living in the center of an open-door family gathering place. We never had the stability or privacy that comes with having a home of our own. The constant stream of aunts, uncles, and cousins coming and going at all hours of the day or night was chaotic. Furthermore, our grandparents and extended family members often spoke fluent Italian making it difficult for me to understand all that was being said.

Unlike my father's battles with alcoholism, which seemed distant and external, my mother's struggles with food and body image felt intimately intertwined with my own. She didn't hide her struggles with compulsive overeating. It was a pervasive presence in our lives.

In a household where overeating was the norm, I found myself lost and confused by conflicting emotions, unable to navigate the complexities of proper nutrition and portion control. These feelings were compounded by the memories of our time together, where food played a central role in our outings with impromptu picnics in the car.

These simple yet precious moments gave us such a sense of being a family of our own. Yet, amidst the joy of these simple pleasures, I couldn't shake the underlying sense of unease and frustration upon knowing that our bond was tainted by my mother's struggles.

The codependent relationship between my parents, their battles with addiction, codependency, and living in such a dysfunctional household left me grappling with feelings of insecurity, confusion, and emotional distress.

From Chaos to Clarity

To break free from limiting beliefs and self-destructive patterns instilled during my dysfunctional childhood, I engaged in self-reflection journaling to understand the impact of my upbringing and acknowledge that my worthiness is not determined by external circumstances or past experiences. I practiced positive affirmations and surrounded myself with supportive individuals to build confidence in myself.

I also learned to embrace vulnerability and trust others by gradually opening up and allowing myself to form authentic connections. This required courage and self-compassion, as I had to confront my fear of rejection and abandonment. I actively worked to change my thought patterns and behaviors by identifying and challenging the limiting beliefs that had held me back for so long.

My daily gratitude practice of cultivating a positive mindset, finding silver linings, and practicing gratitude opened my heart to appreciate life's blessings. It shifted my focus from lack to abundance. I now have meaning and direction in my life. I now set realistic and heart-centered intentions that are aligned with my values and passions.

By embracing vulnerability and gradually opening up to trust others, I discovered the gifts of connection. Building authentic relationships and allowing myself to be seen and accepted has brought me profound healing. Building a supportive network of loved ones has provided me with a deep sense of belonging and emotional support.

Inadvertently I had created a working framework for the newfound sense of purpose, joy, and fulfillment I was experiencing. I called it the five golden keys, which evolved into becoming the G.I.F.T.S. method I share with you in this book.

You know, there's a saying, *"The truth will set you free."* In comparison, I have always believed that we know "our truth" where it gets shaky is trusting that we know what to do with it. Perhaps author and motivational speaker Dr. Steve Maraboli said it best in this quote *"Live your truth. Express your love. Share your enthusiasm. Take action toward your dreams. Walk your talk. Dance and sing to your music. Embrace your blessings. Make today worth remembering."*

His wise words of wisdom speak volumes to the validity of what holding the keys to transformation in the palm of your hand can do for you. One of the most important things I learned on my journey is to have role models that you can look up to and excellent examples of what to strive for. So, let's take a look at the characteristics of a strong family:

Characteristics of a Strong Family

A strong family is the foundation of a healthy society. It is characterized by several key characteristics that contribute to its well-being and stability. These characteristics include:

Communication

A strong family actively listens to each other, expresses emotions openly, and resolves conflicts peacefully. They understand the importance of open and honest communication in creating a harmonious environment.

Support and Encouragement

A strong family has a sense of unity. It provides support and encouragement to each other during difficult times. They are there for each other, celebrating achievements, sharing values, and providing comfort during hardships.

Respect and Boundaries

A strong family respects and values each individual's autonomy, while still maintaining healthy boundaries and expectations. They understand the importance of giving each other space and respecting each other's needs.

Financial Stability

A strong family is financially stable. Each member contributes to the household's income and manages resources effectively. This helps alleviate stress and provides a solid foundation for family well-being.

Quality Time

A strong family prioritizes spending quality time together by engaging in activities that bring joy and bonding. This can include family dinners, outings, or simply being together at home.

Positive Influence

A strong family sets a positive example for their children and influences their behavior and values. They demonstrate honesty, kindness, and respect. They also instill these qualities in their children.

Dealing with Crisis
It Can Happen in the Best of Families

When your family or a member of your family is in crisis, it is important to remain calm and take proactive steps to address the challenges at hand. Consider seeking professional help, such as counseling or therapy, to address the emotional and psychological impact of a crisis. This can provide guidance and support for the entire family. Reach out to support groups, online communities, or friends. Sharing experiences with others can provide comfort and offer different perspectives.

Open and honest communication is vital during times of crisis. Encourage family members to express their thoughts and feelings. Actively listen to each other. Compromise and negotiation can help to resolve conflicts and find solutions.

Be prepared for changes in schedules and routines. Be flexible and understanding. Acknowledge that everyone is going through a difficult time. Be empathetic. Offer emotional support to family members and let them know that you are there for them and willing to help. By embodying the characteristics of a strong family and using these strategies when in crisis, you can navigate difficult times and emerge stronger than ever before.

"A real friend is one who walks in when the rest of the world walks out."
— Walter Winchell

13

Personality Development

Your personality is shaped by a combination of factors that work together to make you who you are. One important influence is genetics as you inherit certain traits from your biological parents. These traits can include things like temperament (whether you're naturally more outgoing or introverted) and your tendencies towards certain behaviors or emotions. Brain chemistry and neurobiology also play a significant role in shaping who you are. Let's explore how these biological aspects contribute to your personality development.

Firstly, genetics refers to the genes you inherit from your parents. These genes influence various aspects of your personality such as temperament, emotional sensitivity, and behavioral tendencies. For example, if you tend to be emotionally reactive or calm, these traits can be partly attributed to your genetic makeup.

Your brain is responsible for regulating your emotions, behaviors, and thoughts. Neurotransmitters, which are chemical messengers in your brain, play a crucial role in influencing your mood and personality. For instance, as you've learned earlier, serotonin is linked to feelings of satisfaction and well-being, while dopamine is associated with happiness, motivation, and reward. Changes in neurotransmitter levels can impact your mood and affect how you experience and express your personality traits. Several factors can affect your neurotransmitter levels:

Stress and Anxiety

Stressful situations can trigger the release of stress hormones like cortisol, which can impact neurotransmitter levels. Chronic stress may lead to imbalances in neurotransmitters such as serotonin and dopamine, affecting mood regulation. This contributes to symptoms of anxiety or depression.

Diet and Nutrition

Certain nutrients play a role in neurotransmitter synthesis. For instance, tryptophan which is found in foods like turkey and bananas is a precursor to serotonin production. A balanced diet rich in essential nutrients supports optimal neurotransmitter function.

Sleep Patterns

Sleep is essential for neurotransmitter regulation and restoration. Lack of sleep or disrupted sleep patterns can affect neurotransmitter levels, leading to mood disturbances and cognitive impairments.

Physical Activity

Regular exercise can boost neurotransmitter levels, including serotonin and endorphins, which are associated with feelings of well-being and happiness. Exercise also helps reduce stress and improve overall mood.

Medications and Substances

Certain medications such as antidepressants and mood stabilizers, work by altering neurotransmitter levels to improve mood and emotional stability. Substances like alcohol and drugs can also affect neurotransmitter function, leading to mood changes and behavioral alterations.

Age, Gender, and Hormonal Changes

Neurotransmitter levels can fluctuate with age and hormonal changes. For instance, estrogen and testosterone influence neurotransmitter function. This affects mood and behavior differently in males and females across their lifespan.

Hormonal Influences

Hormones influence aspects of assertiveness, competitiveness, and nurturing behavior. These chemical messengers produced by glands in the endocrine system regulate various bodily functions, including metabolism, growth, reproduction, and mood. When it comes to personality and behavior, hormones can influence emotions, cognitive processes, and interpersonal relationships in significant ways.

Changes in hormone levels during different stages of life, such as puberty or pregnancy, can affect your mood and behavior. This contributes to your unique personality characteristics. Let's explore some key hormones and their impact on your personality:

Estrogen

Predominantly considered a female hormone (although present in both sexes), this influences mood, cognition, and behavior. It plays a role in emotional regulation by promoting feelings of well-being and enhancing social bonding. Fluctuations in estrogen levels throughout the menstrual cycle or during menopause can impact mood and emotional stability.

Testosterone

Mainly known as a male hormone (but also present in females), is associated with assertiveness, competitiveness, and risk-taking behavior. It influences traits like confidence, ambition, and dominance. This contributes to individual differences in personality traits such as extraversion and aggression.

Cortisol

Cortisol is a stress hormone released in response to perceived threats or challenges. While acute cortisol release helps mobilize energy and resources during stressful situations, chronic stress can lead to prolonged elevation of cortisol levels that impact mood, cognition, and behavior. High cortisol levels are associated with anxiety, irritability, and impaired cognitive function, whereas chronically low levels may contribute to feelings of fatigue and apathy.

Oxytocin

Often referred to as the "love hormone" oxytocin is released during social interactions, intimacy, and nurturing behaviors. It promotes feelings of trust, empathy, and connection, strengthening social bonds and fostering prosocial behavior. Oxytocin levels can influence interpersonal relationships, attachment patterns, and overall emotional well-being.

Serotonin and Dopamine

While primarily neurotransmitters, serotonin and dopamine also play roles as hormones in the body. Serotonin is involved in mood regulation, appetite, and sleep while also influencing personality traits such as emotional stability and impulsivity. Dopamine is associated with pleasure, reward, and motivation while also impacting personality traits related to goal-directed behavior, sensation-seeking, and addiction.

Thyroid Hormones

Thyroid hormones like thyroxine and triiodothyronine regulate metabolism and energy production. Thyroid dysfunction, characterized by imbalances in thyroid hormone levels, can lead to changes in mood, cognition, and behavior. This can affect personality traits such as energy levels, mood stability, and cognitive function.

Adrenaline

Adrenaline hormones are released during the "fight-or-flight" responses. They prepare the body for immediate action in response to stress or danger. Adrenaline and noradrenaline increase heart rate, blood pressure, and alertness, influencing personality traits associated with stress response, resilience, and coping mechanisms.

Hormonal fluctuations, influenced by factors such as age, gender, stress, and health status, contribute to the complexity and variability of your personality. Adopting lifestyle practices that support hormonal balance, such as stress management, adequate sleep, regular physical activity, and healthy nutrition can promote emotional well-being and contribute to a more balanced and resilient personality profile. The two most influential are estrogen and testosterone.

The levels of estrogen and testosterone in both men and women are influenced by biological, environmental, and lifestyle. Estrogen levels in females fluctuate naturally throughout the menstrual cycle and decrease during menopause. In males, estrogen is produced in smaller amounts but still plays important physiological roles. Body weight and fat distribution can impact estrogen levels because fat cells produce a form of estrogen called estrone.

Additionally, hormonal contraceptives and hormone replacement therapy (HRT) can alter estrogen levels in females by introducing synthetic hormones. During pregnancy, estrogen levels rise significantly to support fetal development and then fluctuate during postpartum recovery. Environmental exposures, such as endocrine-disrupting chemicals found in certain products, can also influence estrogen levels.

Testosterone levels, which are typically higher in males than females, are influenced by several factors such as lifestyle. Regular physical activity, particularly strength training and high-intensity exercise can increase testosterone levels. A sedentary lifestyle and obesity may lower them. Nutritional factors including the consumption of essential nutrients like zinc and vitamin D and also play a role in testosterone production. Chronic stress can also elevate cortisol levels, which in turn can suppress testosterone production. Adequate sleep is crucial for maintaining optimal testosterone levels.

Certain medical conditions like hypogonadism or polycystic ovary syndrome (PCOS), as well as medications like steroids or hormone therapies, can also impact testosterone levels. Genetic factors contribute to variations in testosterone levels too, with genetic disorders affecting hormone production or receptor sensitivity potentially influencing testosterone levels. Adopting healthy lifestyle practices, including regular physical activity, balanced nutrition, stress management, and adequate sleep, can support hormonal balance and promote overall hormonal health.

Genetics and Your Environment

It's important to recognize that while these biological factors provide a foundation for your personality, they interact with environmental influences and life experiences. This interaction, known as gene-environment interaction, also shapes your personality over time.

Your early experiences during childhood and the way you were raised, especially how you were cared for by your parents and caregivers play a big role in shaping your personality. For example, if you had a secure and loving attachment to your mom and your dad, or other caregivers, you most likely developed a strong sense of trust and confidence in these relationships. On the other hand, challenging experiences like trauma or inconsistent parenting can impact how you view yourself and others.

Your nuclear family dynamics (nurturing, discipline, and role modeling), extended family, peer relationships, social interactions, and cultural background all play a role. The environment you grow up in provides a context for learning social norms, values, and behaviors. Your interactions with family members, friends, and society influence how you see yourself and how you behave in different situations. These psychological factors and life events throughout your life can impact your personality. Major life changes, like moving to a new place, experiencing loss, or achieving personal milestones shape your development and how you respond to them and future challenges.

Your personality is a unique combination of genetic predispositions, early influences and experiences, cognitive patterns, epigenetic environmental influences, and life events. In addition, psychological defense mechanisms like repression, projection, and denial you adopted to cope with stress and anxiety can influence your personality and behavior patterns.

Realize, though, that your personality is not fixed and can change over time. It is continually influenced by ongoing experiences and personal growth.

Attitude is so Important

What's the difference between a thought and an attitude? The difference lies in their nature and scope within your cognitive and emotional processes.

Thought

A thought is a mental process involving the activation of neural networks in your brain that represent ideas, concepts, or images. Thoughts can be conscious or unconscious. They can range from fleeting perceptions to complex reasoning. They are cognitive events that occur in response to stimuli or triggers from your internal or external environment. Thoughts can be specific and transient, such as thinking about what to have for dinner. Alternatively, they can be more abstract and contemplative, such as reflecting on a philosophical idea.

Attitude

An attitude, on the other hand, is a more stable and enduring evaluation or feeling toward a person, object, idea, or situation. Attitudes reflect your beliefs, values, and emotions. They guide your behavior and responses over time. Attitudes involve a combination of thoughts, feelings, and behaviors that are relatively consistent and organized around a particular target. They are typically shaped by past experiences, social influences, and personal values.

While thoughts are individual cognitive processes that can be transient and diverse, attitudes are more comprehensive and enduring evaluations or orientations towards specific targets. Attitudes incorporate thoughts, emotions, and behaviors. They reflect our predispositions and inclinations toward people, things, or ideas. Thoughts can contribute to the formation or modification of attitudes. Attitudes can, in turn, influence your thoughts and actions in predictable ways. Understanding the distinction between thoughts and attitudes helps you navigate your internal processes and interactions with the world around you more effectively.

Your Thoughts in Action

Of particular interest and for embarking on your healing journey, your thoughts and beliefs can influence your personality in profound ways. The way you think about yourself and the world around you, as well as the coping strategies you use to deal with stress and challenges, contribute to developing your personality.

For instance, if you tend to see things positively and believe in your abilities (optimism), your overall outlook is optimistic, positive, and hopeful. Optimistic thoughts can boost your mood and enhance your sense of self-worth. On the other hand, if you consistently think negative thoughts about yourself or a situation (pessimism), your overall outlook is pessimistic, which can lead to feelings of sadness, anxiety, or low self-esteem.

The way you interpret events and situations in your mind can impact your emotional well-being and overall personality. Your thoughts, beliefs, and inner dialogue play a significant role in shaping your personality and how you interact with the world. They directly affect your emotions.

Your thoughts influence your behaviors and actions. What you think often translates into how you act. For instance, if you believe you can accomplish a goal, you're more likely to take steps toward achieving it. On the other hand, if you doubt yourself or have negative thoughts about your abilities, you might hold back or avoid certain opportunities. Over time, these patterns of thinking and behaving contribute to our personality traits and habits.

Your thoughts also shape your perceptions of yourself and others. The stories you tell yourself about who you are, what you're capable of, and how the world works become part of your self-concept. If you constantly label yourself as shy or outgoing, smart or not-so-smart, these self-perceptions can become ingrained in your personality. Similarly, your thoughts about others influence how you relate to them, including the dynamics of your relationships.

The good news is that you have the power to change your thoughts and, consequently, your personality traits. By practicing self-awareness and challenging negative or unhelpful thoughts, you can cultivate a more positive and adaptive mindset. Techniques like cognitive reframing, affirmations, mindfulness, and self-compassion can help shift your thought patterns toward greater emotional resilience, confidence, and openness. So, the next time you catch yourself in a cycle of negative thinking or self-doubt, try to pause and reframe your thoughts.

Remember that your thoughts are not fixed truths. They are interpretations that can be reshaped over time. By nurturing a more positive and empowering inner dialogue, you can positively impact your personality and enhance your overall well-being. It's all about cultivating a mindset that supports your growth and authenticity.

Personality Disorders

Personality disorders are a group of mental health conditions characterized by persistent patterns of thoughts, feelings, and behaviors that deviate from cultural norms and cause significant distress or impairment in various areas of life. These disorders typically manifest in adolescence or early adulthood, and they can have profound effects on relationships, work, and overall quality of life. Let's explore some common types of personality disorders and their key characteristics:

Borderline Personality Disorder (BPD)

Borderline personality disorder is characterized by intense emotional instability, impulsivity, unstable self-image, and turbulent interpersonal relationships. Individuals with BPD may experience rapid shifts in mood, difficulty regulating emotions, and fear of abandonment. They may engage in impulsive behaviors such as self-harm, substance abuse, or reckless spending.

Narcissistic Personality Disorder (NPD)

Narcissistic personality disorder is characterized by a grandiose sense of self-importance, a constant need for admiration, and a lack of empathy for others. Individuals with NPD often have an exaggerated sense of their abilities and achievements, seek excessive attention and validation, and may exploit others to achieve their goals.

Antisocial Personality Disorder (ASPD)

Antisocial personality disorder is characterized by a disregard for the rights and feelings of others, impulsivity, deceitfulness, and a lack of remorse for harmful actions. Individuals with ASPD may engage in behaviors such as deceit, manipulation, aggression, and disregard for societal norms and laws.

Avoidant Personality Disorder (AvPD)

Avoidant personality disorder is characterized by extreme shyness, social inhibition, feelings of inadequacy, and hypersensitivity to criticism or rejection. Individuals with AvPD often avoid social interactions and may struggle to form close relationships due to fear of negative evaluation or humiliation.

Obsessive-Compulsive Personality Disorder (OCPD)

Obsessive-compulsive personality disorder is characterized by a preoccupation with orderliness, perfectionism, control, and rigid adherence to rules and routines. Individuals with OCPD may have difficulty adapting to change, may be excessively focused on work or productivity, and may struggle with flexibility and spontaneity.

It's important to note that personality disorders can vary in severity and presentation, and individuals with these disorders may experience significant distress or impairment in functioning. The causes of personality disorders are complex and may involve a combination of genetic, biological, environmental, and psychological factors.

Treatment for personality disorders often involves a combination of psychotherapy and sometimes medication to manage specific symptoms. Early intervention and personalized treatment approaches can help individuals with personality disorders improve their quality of life, develop healthier coping strategies, and enhance their relationships and overall well-being.

If you or someone you know is struggling with symptoms of a personality disorder, it's essential to seek professional help from a mental health provider for an accurate diagnosis and appropriate treatment recommendations. With the right support and resources, individuals with personality disorders can work towards recovery and lead fulfilling lives.

While personality disorders can present significant challenges, they do not define your worth as a human being. Beneath the patterns and behaviors lies an innate self that is deserving of compassion, understanding, and unconditional love.

As we explore ways to manage these conditions, we must also nurture a deep sense of self-worth, self-confidence, and self-esteem. These core elements form the foundation upon which lasting growth and healing can take root. In the next chapter, we will go over some important details about self-worth, self-confidence, and self-esteem.

14

Self-Worth, Self-Confidence, and Self-Esteem

Self-worth, self-confidence, and self-esteem are interconnected concepts that relate to how you perceive and value yourself. Although they are related, they have distinct meanings and implications. A healthy sense of self-worth contributes to higher self-esteem and self-confidence. Conversely, low self-esteem or lack of self-confidence can undermine your sense of self-worth.

Self-Worth

Self-worth stems from a deep sense of self-respect and acceptance. You value yourself as a human being and recognize that you are deserving of love, happiness, and fulfillment simply because you are alive. Self-worth is not contingent on external achievements, appearance, or approval from others. You accept yourself unconditionally, strengths and weaknesses included. You acknowledge your imperfections, weaknesses, and vulnerabilities without diminishing your sense of value or self-respect. This acceptance allows you to develop a more balanced and compassionate view of yourself.

Having a strong sense of self-worth often correlates with the ability to establish and maintain healthy boundaries in relationships. This enables you to recognize and assert yourself, stand up for your needs, and values, and defend your rights, without feeling guilty or inadequate. With such a healthy sense of self-worth, you are more resilient in the face of challenges and setbacks. You are better able to bounce back from failures, criticism, or rejection because your self-esteem is not solely dependent on external validation.

You believe in your abilities, possess self-control, and have agency and influence over your own life. You take responsibility for your choices and actions, which contributes to a greater sense of empowerment and autonomy. The development of self-worth can be influenced by early experiences, relationships, and cultural backgrounds, particularly during childhood and adolescence. Positive reinforcement, validation, and support from parents and caregivers play a crucial role in shaping your self-perception and self-esteem.

Building and nurturing self-worth is an ongoing process that requires self-awareness, self-compassion, and intentional practice. This may involve challenging negative self-beliefs, setting healthy boundaries, practicing self-care, and surrounding yourself with supportive relationships.

Self-Confidence

Self-confidence means you believe in your abilities. You believe you possess qualities, and skills with complete competence and trust in your judgment. You believe that you can handle tasks, achieve goals, and navigate challenges in life effectively. Confidence fosters a sense of independence, allowing you to take risks and pursue ambitions. You feel empowered to overcome obstacles with resilience and determination. You face challenges without fear.

This inner assurance is rooted in a positive self-perception and realistic appraisal of your strengths and capabilities. This can come from past experiences, achievements, or positive feedback from people you trust.

As a child, you begin to develop self-confidence that is influenced by various factors, including parental support, educational experiences, and personal achievements. Positive reinforcement and encouragement during these formative years can foster a sense of competence and self-assurance. Conversely, experiences of criticism, failure, or lack of support can undermine self-confidence and contribute to self-doubt. Self-confidence is about having a balanced sense of assurance in yourself. It's not about striving for perfection or being arrogant by thinking you are superior to others.

Perfectionism is the tendency to strive for flawlessness and set excessively high standards, often leading to dissatisfaction and self-criticism when expectations are not met. Arrogance is an exaggerated sense of your importance by a dismissive attitude towards others. Instead, embrace your strengths with humility, and be open to continuous learning and self-improvement. Recognize and appreciate your strengths and positive qualities while also acknowledging areas where improvement or growth is possible. This balanced perspective allows you to feel secure in your abilities without being overly critical of yourself or others.

You acknowledge the things you excel at and take pride in your accomplishments, while also being open to learning, developing your skills, and improving in areas where you may have weaknesses. You possess a growth mindset, viewing challenges as opportunities for learning and personal development.

Building self-confidence is an ongoing process that requires self-awareness, self-acceptance, and intentional effort. It often involves stepping outside comfort zones, setting achievable goals, and celebrating small victories along the way. Self-confidence can be cultivated through skill development, positive self-talk, visualization techniques, and constructive feedback from mentors or peers.

A key aspect of self-confidence is the ability to adapt to new situations and handle uncertainty with composure. Self-confident people are more likely to embrace change, take initiative, and assert themselves in social and professional settings. They exude a sense of authenticity and assertiveness that attracts respect and admiration from others.

External factors such as social comparisons, societal expectations, and cultural norms can influence self-confidence. However, true self-confidence is rooted in internal validation instead of approval or validation from others. It involves developing a strong sense of self-efficacy and resilience, which allows you to bounce back from setbacks and pursue your aspirations with conviction. By nurturing self-awareness and embracing personal growth, individuals can strengthen their self-confidence and lead more fulfilling lives.

Self-Esteem

Self-esteem is subjective and is a self-evaluation of your worth and value, coupled with your self-acceptance, self-respect, and self-love. It is influenced by both your self-worth and self-confidence.

Self-esteem involves evaluating yourself positively and considering yourself worthy and competent. With healthy self-esteem, you tend to have a positive self-image, a realistic favorable view of yourself, and belief in your abilities. You recognize your strengths, accomplishments, and worth. You can embrace your imperfections and limitations without feeling diminished or inadequate.

Your self-esteem is influenced and developed by various factors, including early experiences, interpersonal relationships, societal messages, and personal achievements. Positive experiences such as encouragement, praise, and support during childhood contribute to the formation of a positive self-image and healthy self-esteem. Conversely, experiences of neglect, criticism, or rejection can erode self-esteem and lead to feelings of unworthiness.

Self-esteem is closely linked to self-worth and self-confidence. It plays a critical role in shaping how you perceive yourself and your capabilities. High self-esteem fosters a sense of self-efficacy and resilience, enabling you to pursue goals with confidence and assertiveness. On the other hand, low self-esteem can manifest as self-doubt, fear of failure, and difficulties asserting your needs and boundaries.

Cultivating and maintaining healthy self-esteem requires self-awareness, self-compassion, and intentional self-care practices. It involves challenging negative self-beliefs, practicing self-acceptance, and nurturing supportive relationships. It is an ongoing process that involves recognizing and appreciating your worth and unique qualities.

It's important to differentiate healthy self-esteem from external validation or comparison to others. True self-esteem comes from an internal sense of worth and self-acceptance instead of seeking approval or validation from external sources. By fostering a positive self-image and nurturing self-compassion, you can cultivate a strong foundation of self-esteem that empowers you to lead a fulfilling and authentic life.

Addressing Self-Perceptions
What to Pay Attention to

When addressing your perceptions of self-worth, self-confidence, and self-esteem, remember that while they are distinct concepts, they are closely related nonetheless.

- **Self-worth** provides the foundational belief that you are valuable and deserving of respect.

- **Self-confidence** reinforces this belief by believing in your abilities and skills.

- **Self-esteem**, in turn, combines these two aspects to create a positive self-perception.

Consider the following:

1. **Self-Awareness:** Recognizing and acknowledging your thoughts, feelings, and beliefs about yourself is crucial for developing healthy self-perception.

2. **Positive Affirmations:** Repeating positive affirmations, such as "I am worthy of love and happiness," can help rewire negative thought patterns and improve self-perception.

3. **Setting Realistic Goals:** Setting achievable goals can help you feel more confident and build self-esteem.

4. **Seeking Support:** Surrounding ourselves with supportive individuals who believe in you can enhance your self-perception.

5. **Practice Self-Love and Care:** Taking care of your physical, mental, and emotional well-being is crucial for maintaining a positive self-perception.

6. **Acceptance and Growth:** Being open to feedback and learning from your mistakes can help you grow and improve your self-perception.

As you deepen your sense of self-worth, self-confidence, self-esteem, and respect for yourself and others, you most likely will also recognize the importance of setting healthy boundaries. Boundaries protect your physical, emotional, and psychological well-being while allowing you to engage with others from a place of empowerment rather than depletion. Learning to set clear and compassionate boundaries creates the space necessary for growth, authenticity, and mutually fulfilling relationships.

Setting Personal Boundaries

Boundaries are essential guidelines, rules or limits that we establish to define what is acceptable and unacceptable behavior from others towards us. They are the invisible lines that separate us from others and help us maintain a sense of autonomy, self-respect, and personal identity.

Boundaries play a crucial role in fostering healthy relationships and promoting overall well-being. We need boundaries for several reasons:

Personal Integrity

Boundaries protect our values, beliefs, and principles. They help us stay true to ourselves and prevent others from compromising our integrity or pressuring us into actions that go against our moral code.

Self-Respect

Clearly defined boundaries communicate our self-worth and self-respect. They ensure we are treated with dignity and respect by others. Moreover, they prevent us from being taken advantage of or disrespected.

Emotional and Physical Safety

Boundaries create a safe space around us, shielding us from emotional abuse, manipulation, or physical harm. They allow us to feel secure in our relationships and interactions with others.

Healthy Relationships

Boundaries promote mutual understanding, respect, and accountability in relationships. They set clear expectations and prevent misunderstandings, resentment, and unhealthy dynamics from developing.

Personal Growth

Boundaries encourage self-awareness and self-reflection. By defining what we will and will not accept, we gain a better understanding of our needs, desires, and limitations. This fosters personal growth and self-discovery.

Work-Life Balance

Boundaries help us maintain a healthy work-life balance by separating our professional and personal lives. They prevent us from overcommitting or allowing work to encroach on our time and relationships.

Establishing and enforcing boundaries can be challenging, especially for those who struggle with people-pleasing or have experienced boundary violations in the past. However, setting and maintaining healthy boundaries is an essential aspect of self-care and personal empowerment. It allows you to cultivate fulfilling relationships, protect your well-being, and live a life that aligns with your authentic selves.

The interplay between balance and boundaries is intricate and interdependent. Establishing boundaries enables you to create the necessary space and structure to cultivate balance in your life.

Balance is not a destination but a continuous journey. It's a delicate dance between your personal, professional, and social commitments. It involves intentionally allocating your time, energy, and resources in a way that nurtures your physical, emotional, and mental health. When you embrace balance, you create space for self-care, nurturing relationships, and personal growth. Ultimately. this enhances your overall quality of life.

Boundaries, on the other hand, serve as the guardians of our well-being, protecting you from the relentless encroachment of external demands and internal pressures. They are the lines you draw to define what you will and will not accept, safeguarding your values, beliefs, and emotional sanctuaries. By setting clear boundaries, you communicate your needs, establish healthy limits, and prevent others from exploiting or disrespecting you.

Without boundaries, you risk becoming overwhelmed, drained, and susceptible to burnout. Without balance, your boundaries may become rigid and inflexible, leading to isolation and disconnection.

Achieving this harmonious equilibrium requires self-awareness, intentionality, and a commitment to prioritizing your well-being. It involves learning to say "no" to commitments that deplete you, setting aside time for activities that nourish your soul, and surrounding yourself with supportive individuals who respect your boundaries.

In a world that often glorifies busyness and constant productivity, embracing balance and boundaries may seem counterintuitive. However, it is a courageous act of self-love and self-preservation. By honoring your needs and respecting your limitations, you create the conditions for true fulfillment and joy to flourish.

Ultimately, balance and boundaries are not luxuries. They are necessities for a life well-lived. They are the foundation upon which you build resilience, cultivate meaningful connections, and unlock your full potential. Embrace them wholeheartedly. In doing so, you embrace the essence of your well-being, allowing yourself to thrive in every aspect of your life.

How to Know When to Set Boundaries

Determining when to set boundaries is a personal decision that depends on several factors, including your values, needs, and comfort level. Here are some signs that it may be time to set boundaries:

Feeling Overwhelmed

If you are constantly feeling stressed, exhausted, or overwhelmed, it may be a sign that your boundaries are being crossed.

Feeling Drained

If you find yourself feeling emotionally drained or resentful in relationships, it may be a sign that your boundaries need to be adjusted.

Lack of Self-Care:

If you are neglecting your needs in favor of others, it may be a sign that your boundaries are being violated.

Inconsistent Values

If your values and priorities are being compromised, it may be a sign that your boundaries are unclear or non-existent.

Feeling Enmeshed

If you find yourself feeling trapped or unable to make decisions, it may be a sign that your boundaries are not clearly defined.

Setting Boundaries in the Most Loving Possible Way

Setting boundaries in a way that promotes love, respect, and open communication can be challenging. Here are some tips to help you set boundaries in the most loving way possible:

1. **Communication is Key:** Communicate your boundaries to the other person by using "I" statements and avoiding blame or judgment.

2. **Be Firm but Kind:** Set clear limits while being respectful and considerate of the other person's feelings.

3. **Practice Empathy:** Understand the other person's perspective and validate their emotions before setting boundaries.

4. **Avoid Guilt-tripping:** Avoid making the other person feel guilty for setting boundaries. Emphasize that it is essential for your well-being.

5. **Repeat and Redirect:** If necessary, repeat your boundaries and redirect the conversation if the other person tries to cross them.

Boundaries are essential for maintaining healthy relationships, personal well-being, and emotional balance. By setting boundaries, you protect yourself from burnout, manipulation, and feelings of being overwhelmed. It is crucial to recognize when you need to set boundaries and communicate them in the most loving way possible. Remember, setting boundaries is an act of self-care and love. It is an important step towards creating a fulfilling and meaningful life.

*"In family life, love is the oil
that eases friction,
the cement that binds us closer together,
and the music that brings harmony."
– Eva Burrows*

15

Strengthening Communication

Strengthening your relationships with family and friends is about building genuine connections with your loved ones based on trust, openness, and understanding. It's about being real and honest in your interactions by embracing who you truly are within the relationship.

Adding more meaning and depth to your relationships by being your true self allows others to do the same and creates a powerful connection. You must be willing to share your joys as well as your struggles openly and encourage your friends to do the same. This vulnerability fosters a deeper sense of trust and understanding. When you open up about your fears, insecurities, and joys, it creates a deeper emotional bond. It encourages empathy and support from those you care about.

Embrace Vulnerability

Vulnerability is not a weakness to be avoided or hidden. It's a strength to be embraced. It is a gateway to deeper connection, authenticity, and growth. Vulnerability is the willingness to show up as your authentic self and allow yourself to be seen and heard for who you truly are. It requires the courage to speak your truth, express your emotions, and show up as your true self to the world, even when it feels uncomfortable or risky.

Social media often puts perfection and strength on display, so showing vulnerability feels daunting. We fear rejection, judgment, and criticism. So we build walls around our hearts and hide behind masks. Yet, it is in our moments of vulnerability that we forge the deepest connections with ourselves and with others.

When you allow yourself to be vulnerable, you invite others into your inner world by sharing your hopes, fears, dreams, and true struggles. In doing so, you create space for empathy, understanding, and genuine connection to flourish. It is through vulnerability that you build trust, foster intimacy, and cultivate meaningful relationships that will nourish and sustain you.

Vulnerability is not just about sharing your struggles, it's also about celebrating your joys and successes by allowing yourself to be seen in moments of happiness and triumph. It's about embracing your authentic self in all aspects of life. It's about showing up fully and unapologetically. It's about being unafraid to show the world who you truly are, flaws and all, and finding empowerment in that authenticity.

Stepping into your truth and owning every part of yourself and the journey that has brought you to where you are today is an act of self-love, and acceptance. It's a declaration that you are worthy of being seen and celebrated exactly as you are. Throughout your continued journey, I encourage you to approach it with an open mind and heart. Have the willingness to embrace vulnerability. By doing so, you will not only gain a deeper understanding of yourself, but you will also forge a path toward greater authorship of your life.

As you explore strategies for healing past wounds, rewriting limiting beliefs, and reclaiming your power to create the life you desire I am honored to accompany you every step of the way. I promise you, that no matter how far down the rabbit hole you may feel you have fallen, your light is strong enough for you to see your way out of the darkness. Your inner light is unwavering, resilient, and powerful. It may flicker amidst the shadows, but it never fades completely.

Authenticity and Open Communication

Transparency and honesty are crucial. Avoid hiding your true thoughts or feelings as this can lead to misunderstandings. Practice open communication by expressing yourself authentically and respectfully, even if it means having difficult conversations. Respecting each other's boundaries is essential for authenticity in relationships. Encourage open dialogue about boundaries and preferences. Strive to honor each other's needs and limits. When you respect each other's boundaries, it fosters a sense of safety and acceptance within the relationship.

Celebrating individuality is another way to nurture authenticity. Embrace and appreciate each other's uniqueness. Allow space for personal growth, interests, and aspirations. Encourage each other to pursue individual passions. Supporting each other's individuality strengthens your bonds and adds richness to the relationship.

In addition, prioritize emotional connections by sharing meaningful experiences, memories, and emotions with your loved ones. Create opportunities for heartfelt conversations and expressions of care and appreciation. Building emotional connections deepens your relationship and strengthens the foundation of trust and intimacy.

Prioritize authenticity in your interactions. Once achieved, watch as your relationships thrive with honesty, acceptance, and deeper connections. Always approach conflicts with authenticity and empathy. Conflict is a natural part of relationships, but how you handle it matters. Be real, listen actively, express yourself honestly yet respectfully, and work together to find solutions that honor both perspectives. Resolving conflicts constructively can strengthen your bond and build resilience.

Also, don't hesitate to show appreciation and support. Celebrate others' successes and be there for them during tough times. This kind of genuine care strengthens bonds and makes your relationship more meaningful. Express gratitude for your loved one's presence, support, and contributions within your relationship. Small gestures of kindness and love strengthen your bonds and create a positive atmosphere.

Effective Communication

Effective communication is truly the cornerstone of any healthy relationship, whether it's with family, marriage, children, or with friends. It lays the foundation for understanding, trust, and empathy. Effective communication is the ability to convey thoughts, feelings, information, or ideas clearly and accurately. Moreover it also involves listening actively and empathetically to others. It involves expressing yourself in a way that is understood and received as intended. It's listening without interrupting in a way that shows them that you value their perspective and care about what they have to say.

When you take the time to communicate openly and honestly, you build a sense of intimacy and closeness with your loved ones. This openness encourages them to reciprocate and share their thoughts and feelings as well, creating a two-way street of communication that strengthens the relationship.

Spend some time thinking about your communication skills. The following exercise can help you identify areas you'd like to improve on and what your goals and aspirations are for your relationships.

Self Reflection Exercise

Think about each relationship by naming each person individually as you ask yourself, and journal the following questions for each:

- How do I feel when talking to family members or friends?

Acknowledging these emotions can be the first step towards opening up more effectively.

- Are there topics or feelings that I tend to avoid or find challenging to discuss?

Reflect on what you value and identify areas where deeper communication could strengthen your bonds.

- What topics or conversations have brought me closer together or deepened my understanding of each other?

Reflect on the qualities of these interactions that contribute to a sense of understanding and mutual support.

- Have there been periods in conversations where differences of opinion, or misunderstandings negatively impacted our relationship?

Reflecting on these experiences can reveal areas for potential growth or open-mindedness.

- Throughout my life, have I encountered challenges or barriers in expressing my thoughts or emotions openly and authentically to loved ones?

Consider how not expressing yourself openly has impacted your relationships and identify opportunities for growth and improvement.

- Are there unresolved issues or lingering emotions that I'd like to address through communication?

Reflect on how these issues have impacted your connection with others. Determine whether there are opportunities for open and honest dialogue to address them.

- How often do I actively listen and validate the feelings of family members and friends?

Notice if you tend to listen attentively without interrupting and if you show empathy for their feelings during conversations.

- Do I use "I" statements assertively to express my needs and opinions while respecting others' opinions and boundaries?

Reflect on how you advocate for yourself in relationships while respecting others' opinions and boundaries.

- What do I hope to achieve through improved communication and how do I envision my relationships evolving as a result?

Setting clear communication goals can guide your efforts toward fostering trust, understanding, and connections for healthier, more fulfilling relationships.

- Imagine an ideal conversation with each family member and friend. Ask yourself what it looks like, and how you feel during and after each of these interactions.

Visualizing a positive and meaningful conversation with those you care about, the topics you would discuss, the atmosphere of the interaction, and the emotions you would experience is a wonderful way to set yourself up for successful communications moving forward.

By improving your communication skills, you can enhance understanding, strengthen emotional connections, and navigate conflicts constructively. Good communication helps resolvie conflicts peacefully. When disagreements arise (as they inevitably do in any relationship), engaging in effective communication will allow you to address issues calmly and respectfully.

You must be mindful of expressing your concerns without blaming or accusing them. Actively listen to the other person's viewpoint. This mutual understanding often leads to finding solutions that satisfy both parties and prevent lingering resentments.

A key aspect of effective communication is active listening. Take the time to truly listen to the other person without interrupting or formulating your response prematurely. Show empathy and interest in their perspective before sharing your thoughts or feelings. Expressing empathy is essential for fostering meaningful connections. Put yourself in the other person's shoes and validate their feelings. Ask questions and show genuine interest in their experiences to demonstrate empathy and understanding.

Using "I" statements is an important strategy. Express your feelings and needs using phrases like "I feel..." or "I need..." to take ownership of your emotions. This approach encourages open and honest dialogue while reducing defensiveness and blame.

Nonverbal cues also play a significant role in communication. Pay attention to your body language, eye contact, and facial expressions. Ensure that your nonverbal signals align with your verbal message to convey sincerity and openness.

Incorporate these communication strategies into your interactions with family and friends to cultivate healthier relationships, resolve conflicts more effectively, and create a supportive social environment. Consistent practice of these skills will enhance your communication abilities and enrich your connections with others over time.

Effective communication is about embracing and expressing love and connection authentically. It's about being present, showing empathy, and nurturing these precious connections with family and friends. Remember, it's not about perfection, it's about progress. Every step you take toward building healthier relationships will bring more fulfillment and happiness into your life.

Effective communication is a skill that can be learned and refined. As you apply these techniques in your daily interactions, observe how they positively impact your relationships and overall well-being. Communication is the cornerstone of meaningful connections and plays a vital role in nurturing fulfilling relationships throughout life.

Another crucial thing is spending quality time together. Whether it's having a meal together, going for a walk, or simply chatting over the phone, these moments strengthen bonds.

Dealing with Communication Issues

Dealing with situations where one person in a relationship talks excessively or exhibits shyness can be challenging, especially if it leads to an imbalance in communication or feelings of frustration. Addressing excessive talking and shyness in a relationship requires patience, empathy, and open communication.

Excessive Talking

First of all, it's important to realize the need some people have for talking excessively or taking control of conversations. It stems from various underlying factors related to personality traits, emotional needs, or communication styles. One reason people may feel compelled to dominate conversations is a desire for validation or attention. They may seek affirmation or approval from others through talking, believing that their contributions will make them more visible or significant in social interactions.

Additionally, individuals who talk excessively may use conversation as a means of coping with anxiety or discomfort in social settings. Talking can fill silence or mask insecurities, providing a sense of control and comfort in interactions.

Another contributing factor could be a natural inclination towards extroversion or assertiveness in communication styles. Some individuals are naturally more outgoing or expressive. They may feel energized by engaging in conversation. They may not always be aware of how their communication style impacts others, leading to unintentional domination of discussions.

Furthermore, the need to control conversations can arise from a desire to influence or persuade others. Individuals with strong opinions or leadership qualities may take charge of conversations to steer them toward specific outcomes or decisions. This behavior can be driven by a sense of confidence in their ideas and a belief that they know what's best for you or the group.

To address this issue respectfully and effectively, establish clear boundaries around communication. Express your needs gently to the talkative individual by emphasizing the value of mutual sharing and listening in conversations. Encourage a more balanced dialogue where both of you have the opportunity to contribute and participate actively.

When the talkative person is sharing, practice active listening to demonstrate genuine interest and attentiveness. Use nonverbal cues such as nodding, maintaining eye contact, and interjecting with brief affirmations to convey your engagement in the conversation. These subtle cues can encourage the speaker to feel heard and valued without dominating the interaction.

Another strategy is to redirect the conversation periodically to different topics or activities that allow more inclusive participation. In a group setting, encourage the talkative person to invite others into the discussion by asking open-ended questions or prompting different perspectives. Creating opportunities for shared dialogue fosters a more dynamic and balanced exchange of ideas.

If the imbalance persists and becomes a source of frustration, have an honest and direct conversation about it with the talkative individual. Express your feelings calmly using "I" statements to avoid blaming or accusing. Collaboratively brainstorm solutions that promote equitable communication. Ensure that both individuals feel heard and respected.

Additionally, consider setting time limits for conversations to manage the flow of dialogue more effectively. Agree on specific durations for discussions to allow each person equal opportunities to speak and listen. This approach can help regulate conversation dynamics and prevent one person from dominating interactions.

Above all, approach the challenge with patience, empathy, and open communication to navigate this issue and strengthen your connection with them.

Shyness

When a friend or loved one exhibits shyness to the extent that they struggle to engage in conversation, it often stems from feelings of self-consciousness, anxiety, or discomfort in social settings. Shy individuals may fear judgment or lack confidence in their communication abilities, causing them to withdraw or remain silent in group interactions.

To address shyness effectively, it's important to understand the underlying motivations behind this behavior and approach the situation with empathy and sensitivity. If you are the one feeling uncomfortable being the shy or quiet one during a conversation, embracing self-acceptance is a crucial first step.

Recognize that feeling hesitant or reserved in social situations is a valid aspect of your personality, and everyone experiences unique challenges in social interactions. Gradually exposing yourself to social situations that challenge your shyness by starting with smaller gatherings or one-on-one conversations, can help you build confidence over time. Prepare conversation topics in advance and practice active listening to engage others and shift the focus away from yourself.

On the other hand, if you are seeking to encourage a shy or quiet person to participate more in conversations, creating a safe and supportive environment is key. Foster a non-judgmental atmosphere that allows the shy individual to feel comfortable and valued. Initiate one-on-one interactions to build rapport and establish trust. Listen attentively and show genuine interest in their thoughts and feelings.

Be patient and understanding of their pace and comfort level. Avoid pressuring or rushing them to speak up before they are ready. Offer encouragement and positive reinforcement when they make efforts to participate while acknowledging their contributions and expressing appreciation for their perspective.

By approaching shyness with empathy, patience, and understanding, you can work together to cultivate inclusive and supportive communication dynamics. Celebrate small achievements and progress, as building confidence in social interactions takes time and effort. With mutual support and encouragement, shy individuals can gradually overcome their inhibitions and foster meaningful connections within their relationships.

Addressing Resentments and Cultivating Forgiveness

Realize that we all have our differences and challenges, so showing empathy and being patient with each other can foster a deeper connection. Letting go of resentment and embracing forgiveness to heal old wounds is a transformative process that requires self-reflection, compassion, and willingness to release negative emotions.

Resentment often arises from unresolved hurts, betrayals, or disappointments in relationships. These can cause emotional pain and bitterness over time. To begin, it's important to acknowledge and validate your feelings without judgment. Allow yourself to feel the emotions associated with past wounds. At the same time, recognize that holding onto resentment only prolongs suffering and hinders your personal growth.

Understanding how these feelings manifest, what they reveal about your inner state, and how they impact your overall well-being and relationships is very valuable to the process of letting go of them.

Resentment often develops when you feel hurt, betrayed, or wronged by someone else's actions or words. It can linger and grow over time, poisoning your thoughts and emotions. Resentments can manifest as persistent feelings of anger, bitterness, or hostility towards others, leading to emotional distress and strained relationships.

When someone hurts or betrays you, it can trigger feelings of anger, disappointment, and powerlessness. Instead of expressing these emotions directly, you might have instead internalized them, turning the anger inward by, crazy as it may seem, blaming yourself for the pain you feel.

Blaming yourself for the pain caused by others is often rooted in complex emotional dynamics and cognitive distortions. When someone hurts you, whether intentionally or unintentionally, it can trigger a range of negative emotions such as shame, guilt, or inadequacy. In an attempt to make sense of your feelings and regain a sense of control, you may internalize the blame and attribute the cause to your perceived shortcomings or inadequacies.

One common cognitive distortion that contributes to self-blame is the tendency to personalize external events. You may believe that you are responsible for how others treat you by assuming that their actions are a reflection of your worth or value. This distorted thinking can lead you to overanalyze your behavior or internal state. You will then search for perceived faults or reasons why you deserved to be hurt.

Additionally, societal norms and cultural conditioning may reinforce the tendency to blame yourself for interpersonal conflicts or mistreatment. Messages about personal responsibility and self-reliance can contribute to a sense of guilt or shame when you experience emotional pain in relationships.

Moreover, self-blame may also be a coping mechanism to maintain a sense of control or agency in challenging situations. By attributing the cause of your pain to yourself you may believe that you have the power to change or prevent similar experiences in the future.

However, it's important to recognize that self-blame is often irrational and counterproductive. It can perpetuate feelings of low self-esteem, undermine self-worth, and hinder emotional healing.

To break free from the cycle of self-blame, it's essential to challenge distorted thinking patterns, practice self-compassion, and cultivate a deeper understanding of your inherent worth and value that is separate from others' actions. By reframing your perspective and acknowledging that you are not responsible for others' actions, you can begin releasing self-blame and embark on a journey of self-acceptance and emotional empowerment.

Internalizing resentment can also stem from a desire to maintain relationships or avoid conflict. You suppress your true feelings out of fear of confrontation or rejection, choosing to hold onto resentment as a coping mechanism to protect yourself from further hurt. You may believe that expressing anger or disappointment is unacceptable or weak, leading you to bury these emotions deep inside.

On the other hand, when you hold a grudge against someone and feel resentment towards them without internalizing it, it reflects a different emotional response to hurt or betrayal. Instead of blaming yourself for the pain caused by others, you can externalize your feelings of anger, disappointment, or betrayal towards the person who hurt you.

Holding a grudge can be a way of asserting boundaries or protecting yourself from further harm. It may stem from a sense of injustice or a desire for validation of your emotions. By holding onto resentment, you may seek acknowledgment or accountability from the other person, hoping that they will recognize the impact of their actions and take steps to make amends.

At the same time, holding a grudge may also be of a desire to maintain emotional distance or self-protection. You may use resentment as a shield to prevent further vulnerability or emotional intimacy with the person who hurt you. You may even resort to giving the silent treatment.

Silent treatment is passive-aggressive behavior where you intentionally ignore or withhold communication from another person express displeasure, assert control, or avoid conflict. It can be used as a manipulative tactic to punish or manipulate the other person, leaving them feeling confused, hurt, and anxious. The silent treatment can create emotional distance and undermine trust in relationships, as it prevents open communication and resolution of conflict.

Addressing the silent treatment requires assertive communication, clear boundaries, and mutual respect and understanding within relationships. While holding a grudge may provide a temporary sense of validation or protection, it can also perpetuate feelings of bitterness and negativity over time.

Resentment can erode relationships, increase stress levels, and hinder personal growth and healing. By clinging to resentment, you inadvertently give power to the past. You allow negative emotions to dictate your present state of mind and impact your interactions with others.

Letting Go of Resentments

To address and release resentment towards someone without internalizing it, cultivate self-awareness and explore the underlying emotions driving the grudge. Reflect on the reasons behind your feelings of resentment and consider the impact keeping negative emotions on your well-being.

Practice forgiveness and compassion towards yourself and the other person involved. This does not necessarily mean condoning their actions. Rather it's choosing to let go of the emotional burden of resentment for your peace of mind.

Engage in open and honest communication with the person if possible. Express your feelings assertively and set boundaries if needed. By acknowledging and addressing resentment towards others without internalizing it, you can cultivate emotional resilience, strengthen boundaries, and create space for healing and growth in your relationships and personal lives.

Letting go of resentments requires self-awareness and a willingness to confront difficult emotions. It involves acknowledging the pain caused by past experiences while choosing to release the grip of anger and bitterness. By practicing forgiveness, you can reclaim your inner peace and emotional freedom.

It'sd important to reiterage that forgiveness does not mean condoning hurtful behavior or forgetting past grievances. Instead, it's a conscious decision to prioritize your well-being and mental health by releasing toxic emotions and moving forward with a sense of empowerment.

Cultivating Forgiveness

To cultivate forgiveness and let go of resentments, start by exploring the root causes of your feelings. Reflect on the underlying emotions and beliefs associated with past hurts. Practice self-compassion by acknowledging your pain and validating your feelings without judgment. Consider the perspective of the person who hurt you by recognizing their humanity and capacity for mistakes.

Engage in healing practices such as journaling to process your thoughts and healthy release resentments. Surround yourself with supportive relationships and seek guidance from trusted friends or professionals if needed. Remember that letting go of resentments is a transformative journey that requires patience, courage, and self-love. By choosing forgiveness, you can reclaim your power and create space for healing, growth, and more fulfilling relationships in your life.

People make mistakes, and holding onto grudges because of these mistakes can strain relationships. Learning to forgive and move forward can bring a lot of healing and peace to your relationships. Forgiveness is a powerful act of self-liberation and empowerment. When you choose to forgive, you consciously let go of the emotional burden of anger, bitterness, and resentment that weighs you down.

Forgiveness begins with understanding and acknowledging the pain caused by past experiences. It requires courage to confront difficult emotions and embrace vulnerability. By allowing yourself to feel and process your emotions without judgment, you create space for healing and growth.

Cultivating self-compassion is an essential aspect of forgiveness. It involves extending kindness and understanding to yourself. Recognize that you are worthy of healing and peace. Self-compassion will allow you to let go of self-blame and embrace forgiveness as a gift you give yourself.

Forgiveness involves shifting your perspective towards empathy and understanding. It's about recognizing the humanity and imperfections of others, acknowledging that everyone is capable of mistakes and hurtful actions. By choosing empathy, you open yourself up to healing and reconciliation.

Healing old wounds and adding more depth to relationships, it can be truly transformational. Think of it as a journey of self-discovery and growth. First, let's focus on healing those old wounds from childhood. It's about understanding that the past doesn't define the future. By letting go of the hurt and embracing the healing, you're not just restoring relationships with those who hurt you. It's also freeing yourself from carrying the burden of it. It's about creating space for new, positive experiences to unfold.

Processing old emotional wounds often involves seeking professional support from therapists or counselors who specialize in trauma-informed care. Therapy provides a space for exploring unresolved emotions, challenging negative beliefs, and developing healthy coping strategies to navigate triggers and distressing memories.

By cultivating empathy and understanding towards yourself and those who have caused you pain, you open the door to emotional liberation and inner peace. Engaging in self-care practices such as mindfulness, meditation, and nurturing relationships also supports your healing journey. Taking time to prioritize your physical, emotional, and spiritual well-being helps cultivate resilience and fosters a sense of empowerment.

Ultimately, healing old emotional wounds is a gradual and empowering process that requires patience, self-compassion, and a willingness to embrace vulnerability. By honoring your experiences, practicing forgiveness, and seeking support when needed, you can transform past pain into sources of strength and resilience, paving the way for deeper self-understanding, authentic connections, and a more fulfilling life.

16

Marriage and Family

A happy, loving, and long lasting relationship or marriage is a beautiful union built on a foundation of mutual respect, trust, and unwavering commitment. It is a sacred partnership where two individuals come together, not to lose themselves, but to find a greater sense of wholeness and fulfillment in each other's loving arms.

Our Story

Growing up in a dysfunctional family can leave deep emotional scars. The chaos, lack of support, and missed chances to feel truly understood and valued I think made me feel unworthy crucial love and commitment. When I met my husband, it was like finally finding an oasis amidst a desert storm of chaotic loneliness.

Anchor of Stability and Love

From our earliest interactions, my husband had a grounding presence that allowed me to unmask my authentic self without fear or inhibition. With his quiet strength, deep listening skills, and steadfast acceptance, he created a safe space where I could open up and bloom into the person I was meant to be. Though an outwardly shy man, his actions spoke volumes about his determination to make me feel cherished and worthy of love.

As our relationship blossomed into marriage, our commitment to each other only deepened. Together, we built the family foundation that had been so lacking in my upbringing; one of stability, healthy boundaries, and unconditional love. While I could have easily fallen into the cycle of repeating the dysfunctional patterns of my upbringing, my husband's positive influence empowered me to become the nurturing, emotionally available parent I had longed to have as a child.

In his strong but humble way, my husband taught me through living example that I deserved to be loved completely and that functional family dynamics were possible when built on understanding, respect, and true partnership.

Unlike me, my husband came from a stable and loving family background. His values, instilled from a young age, made him inherently stable and grounded. This stability played a pivotal role in shaping our family dynamics. Together, we wanted to create a home that was nurturing, loving, and supportive. We consciously made decisions that were different from what I had seen in my childhood, ensuring that our family life reflected our values and aspirations.

Through my husband's steadfastness and stability, I learned valuable lessons about creating a nurturing environment for our children. The peaceful center of our relationship became the anchor that kept our new family steady amidst the stormy sea of my painful childhood memories.

Our marriage did not erase the scars of my childhood, but it did rewrite the ending. What could have been a tragic continuation of dysfunction became a beautiful new beginning. With my husband's loving guidance, I re-parented myself into the emotionally mature, attuned wife and mother I had yearned to be. Our relationship is living proof that with unconditional love and commitment to breaking unhealthy cycles, the legacy of dysfunction can be reformed into hard-won peace and fulfillment.

Evolution of Love and Growth

While our marriage provided the bedrock of stability and unconditional love that allowed me to blossom, it was not without its challenges. We did not always grow at the same pace. There were times when I experienced leaps of personal evolution while my husband was content in his steady presence. Ever the supportive partner, he gave me the space and encouragement I needed to spread my wings as a creative soul.

Ironically, it was my mother, the very person whose dysfunctional parenting cast such a long shadow over me, who helped us out financially at times even though she did so by overstepping boundaries we never set. Our weakness in that regard was her gain. As manipulative as her actions were, she did strive to be a loving grandmother to our children, which we were grateful for.

For many years, the sanctuary of our marriage was enough to keep the demons of my disheartened upbringing at bay. I was able to be fully present in raising our family, secure in the knowledge that this was the healthy, nurturing home environment I had always craved.

Parenting Our Four Beautiful Children

Out of the sanctuary of our marriage grew an equally nurturing environment for raising our four beautifully unique children. From the gutsy and witty daughter who kept her brothers on their toes, to our three enterprising sons who each forged their successful paths, we aimed to celebrate and support their individual strengths.

Our parenting philosophy was one of interdependence by providing the loving boundaries and guidance they needed, while also giving them the space and encouragement to challenge themselves, take risks, and develop into self-motivated individuals. Praise, affirmations of our unconditional love, and consistent emotional attunement were our core principles.

Watching each child blossom into the accomplished adults they are today has been an unparalleled joy. All of our children are happily married and raising children, and we couldn't be prouder. Our daughter, now a grandmother herself, is the mama bear of five children, a homeschooling mother, and a hard-working entrepreneur who owned and operated a preschool while raising her first three children.

Our oldest son's childhood computer talents morphed into a thriving computer programming career while being a successful business owner. He is the father of three children. Our self-determined middle son stayed true to his adventurous spirit. He's the father of one son and owns a digital design agency. He and his wife embraced travel early on by becoming expats in another country. Our youngest son also showed entrepreneurial leanings. As a young boy, he would buy and resell sunflower seeds to his childhood friends. As an adult, he worked his way up the corporate ladder where he now manages an entire branch of a company.

While we had our inevitable parenting challenges, we held steady in our commitment to foster close family bonds through life's ups and downs all while empowering each child to pursue their dreams wholeheartedly.

"Attitude is so important" was a term I used often to help our children realize that a positive attitude encourages problem-solving with creativity. I firmly believe that attitude is a fundamental aspect of raising children because it shapes their outlook on life, influences their behavior and interactions, and contributes to their overall well-being and success.

I think the struggles I went through during my upbringing helped me quickly identify behaviors and patterns that alerted me of issues I was able to nip in the bud most of the time because I made a conscious effort to break negative cycles. This led to healthier and more positive parenting practices. We were not perfect parents, and that's a good thing. Even though we tried our best, our children know that it's okay to make mistakes. After all, that is how we learn and grow.

When our children gained their independence, and started families of their own, our roles shifted as our grandchildren arrived. Each one injected new vitality and love into our lives. We delight in being hands-on grandparents as much as we can while recognizing that our babies have grown into nurturing guides themselves.

There is something profound about witnessing the legacy you helped cultivate spread into future generations. Our family has branched outward, with each new branch bearing unique fruit. Yet they all sprouted from the roots we planted of acceptance, empowerment, laughter, and most of all, an abundance of love that conquers all.

A New Season

Life is full of transitions. Now we find ourselves in a new season of our lives. This period of change requires us to continually make adjustments and compromises. It's an important evolution, essential for sustaining the passionate and supportive partnership we have built over the five decades we've been together. Embracing this new chapter with understanding and flexibility will help us maintain the strong bond that has carried us through so many years.

I don't claim to be an expert, and I am sure neither does my husband. However, I would like to share what I have come to know and believe a happy, healthy, loving, and long-lasting marriage consists of.

Strategies for a Healthy, Happy, Long-Lasting Relationship

I believe that at the core of a happy, loving relationship you must be willing to have open and honest communication. Partners need to feel comfortable expressing their thoughts, feelings and needs without fear of judgment or criticism. You need to actively listen to one another. Seek to understand and empathize even when you're faced with differing perspectives. This open dialogue fosters a deep connection and intimacy that transcends the physical realm.

Love, in its purest form, needs to permeate every aspect of your relationship. It is the force that nurtures, uplifts and inspires growth in you both. Love manifests through thoughtful gestures, words of affirmation, and acts of kindness that strengthen the bond between a couple. It is a constant choice to put both of your wants and needs on equal footing to create a harmonious balance of give and take.

Trust is the bedrock upon which a healthy marriage is built. Partners need to be able to rely on each other, knowing that their vulnerabilities will be respected and their secrets kept sacred. This cultivates an environment of emotional safety, where you both can be your authentic selves without fear of betrayal or deception. This trust breeds a sense of security and stability, allowing your relationship to weather life's inevitable storms.

Mutual respect is woven into the fabric of a loving marriage. As partners you recognize and appreciate each other's unique strengths, quirks, and differences. You embrace one another as part of the beautiful tapestry that is your union. You uplift and support one another's dreams, ambitions, and personal growth with the understanding that each of your successes contributes to the collective success of your relationship.

Intimacy, both physical and emotional, plays a vital role in a healthy marriage. As partners, you both feel joy and fulfillment in your physical connection, as you celebrate the depth of your love through tender moments and passionate embraces. Emotional intimacy runs deeper as you share your innermost thoughts, fears, and hopes, creating a haven where you both feel truly known and accepted.

In a happy, loving, and healthy marriage, partners are not merely companions; they are best friends, confidants, and lifelong partners in crime. You share laughter, create cherished memories, and weather life's challenges together, hand in hand. Your love is a constant source of strength, resilience, and inspiration, reminding you that no obstacle is too great when faced with unwavering support and commitment.

R.E.S.P.E.C.T.

My husband and I have a motto that we live by that is the acronym R.E.S.P.E.C.T.

Responsive: As respectful partners you take the time to listen to each other's needs, concerns, and opinions. You actively listen to understand rather than respond impulsively.

Empowered: A respectful relationship is built on the foundation of trust and support. Each of you feels valued and empowered to make decisions and choices that benefit both of you.

Secure: As respectful partners you create and maintain a safe and nurturing environment. You protect each other's privacy, honor boundaries, and prioritize each other's well-being.

Positive: As respectful partners you focus on the positive aspects of your relationship. You celebrate each other's successes, encourage personal growth, and provide emotional support.

Equal: As respectful partners you value equality and fairness in all aspects of your relationship, we treat each other equally, listen to each other's perspectives, and strive to create a balanced partnership.

Choice: As respectful partners you give each other the freedom to make your own choice. We support and respect each other's decisions, even when they don't align with your own.

True: As respectful partners you are honest, authentic, and trustworthy. You follow through on commitments, communicate openly, and support each other's dreams and aspirations.

*"The love of family
and the admiration of friends
is much more important
than wealth and privilege."
– Charles Kuralt*

KEY OF TREASURED WISDOM

Unlock the gift of knowledge and insights that nourish your soul and uncover the treasure trove of generational wisdom collected within yourself, which you are blessed to share with others and contribute to the collective wisdom of humanity.

17

The Key of Knowledge and Insight

As my children gained their independence and as my husband settled into his retirement years, I found myself at a crossroads. The nest was empty, and the hobbies and interests that once fulfilled me no longer seemed enough. Restlessness took root within my soul and I yearned for deeper purpose and personal growth.

It was during this period of introspection that a new passion emerged from an unexpected place. In my late fifties, I made the bold decision to return to school to become a certified health coach. While entering an academic environment after decades away prompted equal parts excitement and trepidation, I was determined to invest in myself and embrace my second act.

The coursework opened my eyes to holistic wellness principles that resonated profoundly within me. I became captivated by learning about the interwoven aspects of nutrition, exercise, mindfulness, and how to help facilitate lasting change in myself and others. Each new concept stoked the fires of my intellectual curiosity and ignited a desire to live my healthiest, most vibrant life possible.

My studies merged seamlessly with my existing zest for an active lifestyle filled with outdoor adventures, clean eating, and mindful living practices. After completing my certifications, I eagerly launched a health coaching practice focused on guiding others to cultivate the same balanced, joy-infused approach to well-being that reinvigorated my mindset. Whether working virtually with clients across the globe or hosting local workshops, I thrived on empowering people to get on the healthy train and become the captain of their wellness journey.

This vibrant new chapter of ambition was about investing in my soul's evolution and embracing a lifestyle of newfound purpose and passion. My health coaching work kept me constantly engaged, curious, and connected in a deeply fulfilling way during an era when many feel adrift without clear roles to step into later in life.

Looking back, making that life-altering decision to return to school is one of the bravest and most rewarding choices I've made. It was a profound reminder that you're never too old to redefine yourself, discover new wells of potential, and ultimately, embark on a path of delivering more light to this world through your gifts and devotions. My health coaching journey awakened reservoirs of energy, excitement, and a sense of accomplishment.

Approaching sixty, my life took some unexpected turns that tested my resilience. When my mother's health began declining, I put my newfound skills into practice by stepping in as her caregiver. Navigating her health challenges with compassion proved to be an incredible meta for the human capacity to rewrite dysfunctional cycles. Some of my greatest personal growth and acts of unconditional love unfolded while caring for my mother during her final years. When age rendered her fragile while her health deteriorated, I became her fiercest advocate and caregiver despite our painful history.

Equipped with my health coaching education, I assumed every medical responsibility with militant dedication. I deciphered treatment plans, our living spaces for her needs, counseled her through procedures, and simply became a reassuring presence during her most vulnerable moments. I showered her with nurturing patience and commitment to well-being which had been so lacking in my childhood.

There were certainly resentments that resurfaced, family conflicts to navigate, and ample opportunities to react to my old narratives about how she failed me. However, I remained steadfast in caring for her needs. My husband was a great source of strength for me as we both welcomed her into our home.

In her waning months, my mother and I arrived at a point of profound peace and heart-rending gratitude for one another. Her passing created vast inner expanses for me to pen my first published book in 2015 titled, "Hurricane LucyA Caregiver's Guide: Navigating the Storm of Caring for Your Aging Parent." It's a book that gets down to the nitty-gritty of the trials and tribulations that we went through while caring for a strong-willed parent.

After experiencing such a deep-felt loss, I realized that confronting generational trauma would be part of the legacy of that chapter in my life. That book was born from a strong desire to share my experiences and pass on the lessons of strength and emancipation in hopes of benefiting others.

Spreading my Wings

Traveling to Europe had been one of my lifelong dreams. I happened upon an opportunity to be hosted by families looking for a native English-speaking adult from America to come to their home to help their children with their English as a second language skills. I jumped at the chance, promoting myself as a Travel Grandma and offering my services in exchange for room and board. I was able to travel to several different countries by myself this way. My husband also decided to join me in Italy. During the month we were both there, we took a cruise to Greece.

Shortly after returning home, I was hit by another curveball: a diagnosis of colon cancer. Initially, I diligently followed the natural "let food be thy medicine" and related well-documented approaches, believing strongly that my body is capable of healing itself. After all, that's what I had been taught. In fact, years earlier, I had done an internship at the Kushi Institute in Becket, Massachusetts, a macrobiotic education center studying the macrobiotic diet's effects on cancer and disease.

But when further tests revealed that the tumor was growing, I felt disillusioned. I felt my body had let me down, so I opted to have it surgically removed, Thankfully, they successfully got it all with no further treatment required. I felt so defeated and disappointed in the natural health field that I had grown to trust and believe in so much, so hung up my hat as a health coach.

It was during my recovery time at home that I stumbled across van life videos online and felt an undeniable pull. A couple years later I took the plunge. With my husband's blessing, we sold our RV and purchased a minivan to convert into a tiny camper. I kept the name "Travel Grandma" to launch a YouTube channel eagerly joining the van life community as a part-time solo female traveler. I enjoyed many adventures and met so many wonderful people along the way as the open road and nature's song beckoned me to come and play.

It was during this transformative journey of self-discovery that the seeds for this very book you're holding were planted. The vision for this powerful work is aimed at helping others confront their demons, rewrite the narratives that have been weighing them down, and reclaim their power.

From the depths of childhood despair to breaking the cycle of family dysfunction as a wife and mother, my journey has been one of profound transformation. As an empty nester, I boldly reinvented myself through education and then became my mother's caregiver, battled cancer, and found freedom in embracing van life. This path led me to a soul-reckoning about my roots. These experiences have fueled my desire to help others navigate the storms of their own lives.

While the future remains unwritten, I move forward with renewed clarity that my life's highest calling is to share the lessons learned from my resilience. I hope to inspire others to cultivate their fierce self-determination.

Now in my golden years, I've returned to coaching in pursuit of helping others emerge victoriously from the generational cycles and old narratives that once constrained them. By coming home to our worthiness, we can finally unfurl our wings and take flight on our self-defined, soaring journey of passion and purpose.

In the next chapter, I invite you to be the captain of your ship. Take the helm as you embark on a journey to unlock the gift of treasured wisdom that the world is waiting for you to share. Aboard your vessel, named the "Golden Harmony," you will find a treasure map and a compass to guide you. Ahoy, my friend! Bon Voyage on your upcoming journey. Fair winds and following seas to you.

"Wisdom is the ability to discern what is of true value in life."
— Confucius

18

Journey to Unlock Your Treasured Wisdom

Your MISSION, should you choose to accept it is to go on a quest to unlock your treasure chest of knowledge and wisdom to discover the life-changing GIFTS within.

Imagine yourself at the helm of a sturdy ship named the "Golden Harmony" embarking on an exciting adventure across the vast open seas. Guided by a treasure map and compass, you sail toward a mystical island steeped in legend. It's a sanctuary said to hold valuable treasures of wisdom that are left for you to discover.

The salty ocean air invigorates your senses. The ocean spray gently touches your skin with each rolling wave. What you're embarking on is far from an ordinary treasure hunt. The prize that awaits you on that legendary island is a collection of generational wisdom. It contains insights passed down by those who came before while being carefully hidden away in a sealed chest.

As the rugged cliffs of the island come into view, you feel the weight of the mysterious golden key tightly clutched in your hand. You discovered this key as a young child while wandering along the beach collecting seashells as your mind was filled with wonder and curiosity. Washing ashore amidst the waves, you spotted a bottle containing this ancient, ornate key. From that moment, you sensed its significance It's a special golden key meant for you to find, and you are destined to unlock an amazing treasure trove of wisdom when the time is right.

Throughout the years, as you navigated life's journey, each experience, lesson learned, and challenge overcome became part of your personal treasures. From the wonderstruck days of childhood to loves found and lost, children born, dreams pursued, storms weathered, and mountains climbed, each milestone enriched your collection of treasures.

Now, as you steer the ship toward the island shore with the golden key in hand, you realize that the treasures you've gathered throughout your life must be like the very gems waiting to be unlocked by the profound wisdom woven into the fabric of your existence. With anticipation and gratitude, you dock your ship and make your way across the shore of the tropical island where an ornately carved chest awaits. It's lid is sealed tight, waiting for you to unlock the secrets that will illuminate your path ahead.

As the secret golden key turns within the lock, it opens to reveal a brilliant cache of multi-colored gemstones. In your hands, these gems begin to transform. They shed their rigid edges as your resilient spirit's optimism works to reveal their true radiant form. What was once the jagged pain of sorrow's cutting edges now refracted into a prismatic light of gifts you have come to understand can also help others endure life's darkest nights. You were able to transform the weight of adversity's burdens into luminous pearls containing solutions for life's irritating problems. One by one, the gemstones morphed into gleaming multi-faceted jewels, radiating kaleidoscopic wisdom, guidance, and echoes of your healing journey.

As these treasures transform into their highest potential before your eyes, you suddenly realize this is not just an exploration for you. It's also a new beginning and the awakening to your higher purpose moving forward. You have reached the sacred core of your being, ignited by the generational wisdom passed down through ancestors before you. Now, this essence flows through you to spread like seeds across the world, nurturing wisdom wherever it finds fertile ground.

You carefully examine each magnificent jewel and its teachings. Perhaps, you can share these recorded words, artistic creations, or shared communities widely as these are not gems to hoard. Instead they are an infinite inheritance to share freely with all. Only you can authentically radiate the unique gifts of insights drawn from the entirety of your remarkable life's journey.

No one else on earth can replicate or replace what only your spirit can emanate, just as how no other being could have produced this uniquely refracted spectrum of truths and knowledge. This wisdom is deeply encoded with the revelations and missions that are mos meaningful to your soul.

As you envision bringing each jewel's gifts to life through ideal means, a profound inspiration takes shape. This is your moment to embrace your role as a beacon of wisdom in today's world. The experiences and gifts of wisdom you've gathered on this island have nurtured your growth as a communicator. They were tasked to guide those seeking deeper understanding.

The treasures within you are not for hoarding but for sharing, to bring healing and inspiration to our world. Like a gift passed down through generations, you're now ready to pass on this enlightened legacy. These 'gems' of wisdom aren't just ordinary. They hold vital truths needed for humanity's progress. Your unique life journey has distilled these gifts of insight. Now, it's your turn to share them with others who crave your perspective.

You possess a special ability for imparting wisdom using modern tools. Whether through digital platforms to share videos and online courses, creative endeavors in writing or artwork, energetic gatherings and community engagement, or personal interactions, you have the skills to make a real impact with your insights.

Your mission is to shine a light so others can find clarity and reconnect with their inner wisdom. We're all interconnected in this quest for knowledge and growth, eagerly awaiting the unique wisdom you're here to share. Know that this wisdom, passed down through the ages, flows through you. Let it infuse everything you do and illuminate the paths of those who benefit from your brilliance and guidance.

This island marks the beginning of your awakening to your new purpose in life as a guiding light rooted in integrity and resilience. Prepare yourself to freely share your soul's treasures wherever they're needed most. The eternal call of discovery awaits you. As a lighthouse of wisdom, radiate your unique insights to enrich our collective understanding and progress in this shared human journey.

As you prepare to share your hard-earned wisdom with the world, it's crucial to remember that your mind, body, and spirit must be cared for and nurtured. The path ahead may be filled with challenges and demands. Maintaining a deep sense of self-love and commitment to your overall well-being will be essential. In the next chapter, we'll explore practical ways to cultivate self-care practices that will fortify your resilience, replenish your energy reserves, and ensure you can sustainably radiate your light without burning out.

Just as a lighthouse requires constant tending and maintenance, so too must you prioritize your needs, boundaries, and inner peace. With a strong foundation of self-compassion and self-nurturing habits, you'll be better equipped to serve as the beacon of wisdom this world so desperately needs.

19

Envision Your Best Day Ever

Before we dive into exploring the essential practices of self-love and self-care, let's first determrnine your "why." Why is it so important to prioritize caring for your own needs? What's the pay-off? By crafting a vivid vision of what your absolute best day would look and feel like, you'll tap into the deep motivation required to instill new habits.

Similar to the vision board you crafted earlier, envision your best day ever as an hour-by-hour experience. This rich, descriptive narrative will bring your overarching visions and goals to life in a tangible way.

Your best day is a glimpse of your highest potential. It is a day when you are firing on all cylinders, filled with vibrant energy, clarity, and joy. It's the experience of being fully immersed in a state of bliss, presence, and alignment with your authentic self. Whether that means spending quality time with loved ones, pursuing a passion project, being in nature, or simply relishing feelings of inner peace and contentment. Get descriptive.

What would the morning routine be that would set a positive tone? How would you fuel your body with nourishing foods? What activities or experiences would engage your mind, stretch your abilities, and light you up? How would you move your body in celebration of its strength and capabilities? Who would you surround yourself with that would uplift your spirit? What small pleasures and simple joys would you savor?

Don't hold back. Dream big. This envisioning exercise is an act of giving yourself permission to imagine your life's full potential for fulfillment and flourishing. After all, how can you expect to achieve profound states of being if you can't envision what they'd feel like?

Describe this day in lush, multi-sensory detail. How would the air feel on your skin? What beauty would you take in with your eyes? What comforting scents, melodic sounds, and delightful tastes would envelop you? Get your creativity flowing by prompting yourself with these types of evocative sensory details.

Once you can vividly picture and embody the experience of your best day ever, let it serve as a beacon, calling you forward. This is your "why" for self-love and care. Because the person experiencing that extraordinary day is the highest manifestation of you through devotion to your well-being, that exceptional person is awaiting your commitment to make the journey to greet them.

So, spend some time now artfully designing and capturing the vision of your most outstanding, joyful day. Allow your heart to guide the narrative as you write it all down in your journal. Let it inspire you with the possibility. Reconnect with this vision frequently to reignite your motivation for self-nurturing for this level of sublime daily experience is well within your grasp through the self-love practices we are about to explore. Here's a simple outline for you to follow:

1. **Set the Scenic Stage**

    Describe the moment you wake up. Be as descriptive as you can about the soft hues of dawn, the comforting surroundings of your bedroom, and the gentle rustle of the morning breeze as perhaps you open a window to let in fresh air. Picture the atmosphere that sets the tone for your perfect day.

2. **Envision Joyful Activities**

   Outline the activities that bring a smile to your face and ignite your passion. Whether it's a serene morning meditation, a creative project, or quality time with loved ones, let your imagination dance with possibilities.

3. **Evoke the Emotions**

   As you write, dive into the sea of emotions you experience throughout the day. Feel the warmth of genuine connections, the thrill of personal achievements, and the tranquility of moments spent in solitude. Allow your heart to guide this narrative.

4. **Reflect on Personal Growth**

   Highlight the moments of personal growth and accomplishment. Visualize and write about overcoming challenges with resilience. Boast about your victories, both big and small. This is your story of triumph, where you emerge stronger and wiser.

5. **Immerse Yourself in Gratitude**

   Conclude your best day story by immersing yourself in gratitude. Express appreciation for the people, experiences, and even the challenges that contributed to this extraordinary day. Let the spirit of thankfulness be the anchor of your narrative.

Writing your best day story is more than a creative exercise. It's a powerful manifestation tool. As you narrate the contours of this remarkable day, you pave the way for its realization.

*"Sometimes the smallest step
in the right direction
ends up being the biggest step
in your life."
- Steve Maraboli*

KEY OF SELF-LOVE & CARE

Unlock the gift of prioritizing self-care
and embracing self-compassion.
Through nurturing these practices,
you cultivate a deep sense of worthiness
and inner peace, which enables you to show
up more fully for others and contribute
positively to your community and the world.

20

Nurturing the Gift of Self-Love & Care

Self-love & care are the foundations for well-being. Without taking the time to nurture yourself holistically, you cannot hope to thrive and live your life to the fullest potential. At its core, self-love & care is about being attuned to your needs across the physical, emotional, mental, and spiritual realms. It's what the five golden keys are built upon. In this chapter, the focus is to build the foundation for a daily self-love and care practice that works on autopilot.

On a physical level, practices like proper nutrition, hydration, exercise, and restorative sleep are critical for fueling your body with vitality. Emotional self-care encapsulates the art of self-awareness by releasing emotional blocks, and honoring your feelings healthily. Mentally, you must "exercise" your mind through stimulation and disconnect from demands when needed. Spiritually, connecting to your deeper values, beliefs, and sense of purpose nourishes your soul. Sound familiar?

Each of these areas influences and impacts the others. An imbalance in one area throws the entire system out of equilibrium. This is why a piecemeal approach is inadequate. True well-being arises from addressing yourself holistically, as an integrated and multifaceted human being.

I mentioned earlier that I am a certified holistic health coach. While my "Health Coach Elaine" business was established with a focus on nutrition, my training at the Institute for Integrative Nutrition included all aspects of well-being as an board certified practitioner by the American Association of Drugless Practitioners. Aside from this coaching practice, I worked with young adults who are on the autism spectrum as an Occupational Counselor for the State of California to teach independent living skills and help them to transition from living at home to living on their own.

Other certifications I hold include Reiki, EFT, Reflexology, American Red Cross BSI and Water Safety Instructor, AFAA Aerobics and Fitness Association of America as a Physical Trainer, and going way back, a Family and Consumer Studies ECE Early Childhood Education Certified Private Agency Preschool Teacher and Director. Yes, while raising our children, I owned and operated Building Blocks Preschool in several locations throughout southern California. So, I've been around the block for quite some time in the education field.

Much of what I share in this self-care section I wrote was part of "The H.E.A.L. Approach: Healthy Eating Active Lifestyle" book series I was doing back in 2015. I published two small pocketbooks, one titled "Self-Care Daily Routine: 10 Easy Ways to Take Better Care of Yourself" and the other titled "Kick Your Sugar Cravings." So, these are not new concepts, but I like to think of them as the natural, sturdy wood set of building blocks you played with as a kid that withstand the test of time.

Neglecting self-care leads to imbalances, burnout, and disease. When you're running on empty physically and mentally while being emotionally overextended, you simply don't have the resources to function optimally. Fatigue, anxiety, and irritability set in such that your work, relationships, and overall quality of life would suffer tremendously.

Self-care is the antidote to the absence of well-being. Beyond just surviving, committing to a holistic self-care practice allows you to thrive and operate from a place of wholeness and abundance. It enables you to respond to your calling, honor your life's purpose, and live each day with vibrancy. Self-care is sometimes viewed as a selfish indulgence, but it's actually the most profound form of preventative self-preservation. It's an investment in sustaining your ability to fully show up for every aspect of your life.

Self-care is radical self-love in action. It's a tangible way you can cherish your mind, body, emotions, and soul as precious resources requiring tender care and devotion. True self-love goes beyond a warm feeling. It's a state of being that you treat with the same compassion, kindness, and care you would show to someone you deeply love.

Self-love requires going inward to understand your authentic needs, boundaries, and intrinsic worth. It's recognizing that you alone are ultimately responsible for nurturing your wholeness. Self-love allows you to stop seeking validation or fulfillment externally. It pushes you to start parenting yourself with patience and unconditional acceptance.

From this wellspring of self-love flows the commitment to care for yourself fully through an ongoing self-care practice. Self-care becomes an outpouring of cherishing all parts of your humanity. When you act from a place of deep self-love, self-care rituals transform into loving gifts and sacred acts of reverence you give yourself.

Self-love reminds you that you are precious and worthy of tenderness. Your mind, body, and soul deserve to not just survive, but thrive. Self-love gives you the courage to prioritize your needs without guilt, knowing that you must first fill your own cup before you can generously pour into the lives of others.

Self-love is being attuned to your feelings and your soul's calling while honoring yourself through compassionate self-care. Only through cultivating deep, unwavering self-love can you build the strong, grounded self-care foundation that allows your overall well-being to blossom sustainably. Self-love is understanding that by caring for yourself devoutly, you're not just filling a need. You're also living in reverence to the precious gift of your humanity.

While cultivating self-love and treating yourself with kindness provides an essential foundation, putting that intention into consistent action is key to living a truly balanced, holistically well life. Establishing a regular self-care practice that nurtures your mind, body, and spirit can help you build resilience, reduce stress, and maintain your overall well-being.

Just as airlines instruct you to secure your oxygen mask before assisting others, prioritizing your self-care practices allows you to show up more fully for all other areas of your life. Whether it's setting aside time for meditation, gentle movement, creative expression, journal writing, or simply pausing to take some deep breaths, engaging in self-care practices sends a powerful message to yourself that you are a priority.

Creating a strong self-nurturing care plan empowers you to live life to your highest potential by being energized, resilient, focused, and attuned to your deepest joys and gifts. Establishing a care plan can serve as a solid bedrock that your overall well-being would be built on. It enables you to blossom into your most vibrant self. When you nurture yourself through self-love & care practices, you can more fully nurture your family, community, and the world we all live in. It all starts from within. The key is to design a self-nurturing care plan with activities that allow you to feel most centered, grounded, and rejuvenated. Next, let's dive into the fundamental pillars of your well-being.

21

Adopting a Rejuvenating Sleep Ritual

I want to start with sleep because studies show that especially in today's day and age, prioritizing a consistent sleep schedule is paramount to everything else you will be doing to get into the rhythm of establishing your care plan. Sleep is an absolute biological necessity that impacts every aspect of mental, physical, and emotional well-being.

In our modern culture consumed by endless digital distractions and the relentless pursuit of more things, quality sleep has become dangerously undervalued and sacrificed. The consequences of cutting corners on restorative sleep resonate through every facet of our lives in harmful ways. Lack of quality sleep is quite literally shortening our lives little by little, and it's time we reclaim this rejuvenating process as the fundamental pillar of self-nurturing care that it truly is.

Let's start on the physical front, where insufficient sleep ravages our bodies like a wrecking ball. Chronic sleep deprivation disrupts the finely tuned dance of our hormones which regulate metabolism, appetite, muscle development, and fat storage. With out-of-whack hormones, our bodies don't process glucose properly. They would crank out excess insulin that triggers inflammation and lays the groundwork for obesity, diabetes, and other diseases.

Lack of sleep also undermines our immune function by limiting our production of infection-fighting antibodies and cells that attack viruses and bacteria. Studies show that people who sleep fewer than 6 hours are four times more likely to catch a cold when exposed to a virus. Plus, sleep is crucial for healing wounds, repairing cellular damage, clearing out neurotoxins, and maintaining a healthy gut microbiome. Losing sleep is essentially pulling the plug on our body's regeneration station.

Insomnia

But the physical ramifications are just the tip of the sleep deprivation iceberg. Mentally, chronic insomnia creates a sputtering, unfocused, and foggy state akin to being drunk. Concentration, decision-making, problem-solving, and memory all become severely impaired. Academic and workplace performance plummet as you lose the cognitive horsepower to fully show up and thrive. Even a single night of poor sleep is enough to trigger irritability, mood swings, depressive symptoms, and struggles with emotional regulation the following day.

Over time, persistent insomnia and sleep disorders contribute to serious mental health conditions like anxiety disorders and clinical depression. Your ability to cope with stress disintegrates, leaving you vulnerable to addiction and other self-destructive compulsions that come as sleep-starved efforts to numb out and escape. Tragically, insomnia is also a prime risk factor for suicide.

Despite the many harmful effects, a surprising 35% of adults say they get less than the recommended 7 hours of sleep. For many, insomnia has become a widespread nightly struggle, perpetuated by habits like:

- Inconsistent sleep/wake times
- Screen exposure from electronics that disrupts melatonin production
- Consumption of caffeine, alcohol, or heavy meals too close to bedtime

- Poor sleep environment due to factors like light, noise, or uncomfortable temperature
- Excessive mental stimulation and an unrelaxed nervous system at night
- Unaddressed underlying conditions like sleep apnea, anxiety, depression, or chronic pain

But here's the crucial piece. While these various obstacles can impair your sleep patterns, all the other factors related to insomnia can become a vicious, self-perpetuating cycle. The longer you lose sleep, the harder it becomes to remedy.

Again, insomnia can arise from a variety of factors including high levels of stress, anxiety, and worry that prevents the mind from quieting down at night. Underlying mental health conditions like depression and anxiety disorders are common insomnia culprits. Medical issues ranging from chronic pain, asthma, and hormonal changes to sleep disorders like sleep apnea and restless leg syndrome can severely disrupt sleep quality. Poor sleep habits like irregular schedules, late-night screen time, caffeine consumption, and the lack of a wind-down ritual enable insomnia. Major life transitions, certain medications, and stimulants like nicotine and alcohol can also contribute to persistent sleep difficulties. While improving sleep hygiene can help, addressing any medical or psychological root causes is key to overcoming insomnia and achieving truly restorative sleep.

And this is why replenishing quality sleep must be the fundamental starting point on your path toward holistic self-care and well-being. Every other noble self-nurturing effort, be it diet, exercise, mindfulness, or anything else, operates at a suboptimal level when we're running on empty from sleep deprivation.

Adopting Five Simple Steps to Better Sleep

So where to begin? Start by adopting these five simple ritualized steps:

1. Avoid stimulants like caffeine, alcohol, and electronics 2 hours before bed.

2. Create a sleep sanctuary environment that's cool, dark, quiet, and comfortable.

3. Engage in relaxing light body stretches, breathwork, or a warm bath

4. Keep a worry journal by your bed to jot down any thoughts that keep you awake

5. Stick to a consistent sleep/wake schedule, even on weekends

If you are unable to fall asleep within 20 minutes, get out of bed and do something calming such as read a book for 5 or 10 minutes and then try again. By treating your sleep like the sacred, non-negotiable form of care that it is, you will benefit more from all the other self-nurturing practices you wish to commit to doing for your overall well-being. But as your first step, sleep is the foundational building block necessary that empowers your entire care plan to thrive most vibrantly.

22

Healthy, Mindful Eating Habits

What you eat is such a hot topic. There are so many different eating plans to choose from but the bottom line is to always eat more whole foods and less processed foods. Digestion starts even before you get the food into your mouth. As you take in the aroma of a freshly prepared meal made with high-quality ingredients, your salivary glands begin releasing enzymes to kick off the digestive process. Eating with this kind of mindful awareness and appreciation for whole, nutrient-dense foods sets you up for optimal nourishment.

Nutrition

A balanced diet rich in whole foods provides your body with the vitamins, minerals, antioxidants, fiber, and other vital nutrients it needs to function at its best. Prioritize eating plenty of fruits, vegetables, whole grains, lean proteins, healthy fats, and drinking sufficient water. These minimally-processed foods deliver maximum nutritional value.

On the other hand, highly-processed and pre-packaged foods tend to be stripped of nutrients and often contain excess sodium, added sugars, unhealthy fats, artificial additives, and empty calories. Frequently consuming these foods can lead to inflammation, sluggish digestion, weight gain, increased disease risks and feeling generally unwell over time.

Beyond just eating nutritious whole foods, promote healthy digestion by focusing on a relaxed eating environment, chewing thoroughly, avoiding excessive liquid intake with meals, and not rushing through your food. Eat slowly and mindfully to naturally tune into your body's satiety cues.

A nourishing diet also depends on choosing the right foods for your individual needs and sensitivities. Work on discovering which whole food groups make you feel energized versus sluggish after eating. Emphasize foods that are seasonal, locally sourced, and as close to their natural state as possible.

Eating this way takes some effort but provides endless benefits, from boosting immunity and managing weight to improving cognitive function and promoting longevity. When you develop a diet based primarily on whole, minimally processed food sources, you'll be rewarded by feeling vibrantly healthy from the inside out.

Mindful eating begins even before you start cooking. Make a meal plan and grocery list beforehand to shop intentionally. As you walk the aisles, become aware of the foods you're selecting and read ingredient labels. Opt for whole food items with minimal and familiar ingredients you can pronounce. Load up on fresh organic, and locally sourced produce, along side lean protein. Organic grass-feed meats and organic free-range eggs, whole grains, legumes, nuts and seeds, and natural spring water are preferred. Let the vibrant colors and aromas engage your senses.

Purchase a wide variety of colored produce. Eating a rainbow of vegetable colors is one of the best ways to ensure you're getting a wide spectrum of vitamins, minerals, antioxidants, and other beneficial plant compounds. Different pigments indicate the presence of different powerful phytonutrients. Allow me to put my geek hat on for a minute to make you aware of the following benefits:

Red Vegetables

Tomatoes, red peppers, beets, radishes, and red onions are rich in lycopene and anthocyanins which can help reduce inflammation. They may also protect against certain cancers and heart disease.

Orange/Yellow Vegetables

Carrots, sweet potatoes, winter squash, and yellow peppers are loaded with beta-carotene and vitamin C. These act as antioxidants and support healthy vision and immune function.

Green Vegetables

Dark leafy greens like spinach, kale, collards, and broccoli are nutritional powerhouses packed with folate, vitamin K, magnesium, and anti-cancer compounds like sulforaphane and indoles.

Purple/Blue Vegetables

Eggplant, purple cabbage, purple potatoes and purple asparagus get their deep shades from anthocyanin antioxidants that protect cells from damage and may boost brain and heart health.

White Vegetables

Onions, cauliflower, mushrooms, and garlic contain flavonoid antioxidants like quercetin as well as sulfur compounds that may help fight cancer and cardiovascular disease.

The more varied your vegetable intake, the more complete the nutritional profile you'll consume. Aim to eat vegetables from as many color categories as possible each day. This rainbow assortment provides complementary combinations of vitamins, minerals, fiber and phytochemicals that work together to maximize health benefits.

In addition to vitamins and minerals, colorful vegetables deliver antioxidants that help protect against cellular damage from free radicals.

The variety of antioxidants in different colored vegetables like vitamin C, carotenoids, and flavonoids, allows them to work synergistically in powerful ways. Strive to purchase and incorporate as many colors as you can at each meal for a broad array of micronutrients that fight inflammation and disease while supporting overall vitality.

Bring reusable bags and buy bulk items to minimize packaging. Once home, extend your awareness into how you store and prepare foods. Refrigerate or freeze perishable food promptly in airtight containers. Storing produce unbagged allows optimal air circulation. Practice FIFO (First In, First Out) for all foods including canned and packaged goods.

Notice the textures, smells, and even the sounds, including sounds from chopping vegetables on a cutting board as you start preparing your food. It's best to wash and chop fruits and veggies yourself versus buying pre-cut. Flash-frozen fruits and vegetables will retain their nutrients just as long as you don't overcook the veggies.

Knife Skills

Arrange a beautiful display of prepped nutritious ingredients on your cutting board as you start cooking. Use proper knife skills like the claw grip, rock chopping, and julienning. Here are some written instructions for these proper knife skills, and there are plenty of online videos demonstrating these techniques as well.

The Claw Grip

This grip protects your fingers while chopping. To do it:

1. Curl your fingers inward to form a claw-like shape
2. Use the knuckle part of your fingers to curl over and guide the food item
3. Tuck your fingertips securely against your knuckles

4. Use your claw hand to grip and guide the food while chopping with the other hand

Rock Chopping

This technique allows you to chop ingredients efficiently. To do it:

1. Use the claw grip to hold the food item steady on a cutting board
2. Grip the knife handle with your other hand with knuckles facing the blade
3. Lift the knife a few inches and bring the blade down at a 45-degree angle
4. Put your weight into rocking the blade back and forth to chop the food

Julienning

This creates thin, uniform strips that are great for salads, stir-fries, etc.

1. First julienne by slicing food into long quartered logs or planks
2. Lay each plank on its side and slice lengthwise into long strips
3. Gather the strips and cut across them with a rocking motion to julienne
4. Go slowly and adjust food grip as needed to maintain even strips

Tips:

- Use a large, sharp chef's knife and start with a good cutting board
- Tuck in your thumbs to avoid injury and anchor the claw hand with your pinkie
- Angle the knife blade towards your body slightly for smoothest cuts

- Go slowly at first until you build up knife skill confidence

With proper techniques like these, you gain more control, efficiency and safety when prepping ingredients. Take your time to develop these essential knife skills in preparation for cooking.

Cooking Techniques

Develop an appreciation for the art of cooking by practicing basic techniques like sautéing, roasting, steaming, and more. Here's how:

Sautéing

Sautéing involves cooking food quickly in a small amount of hot oil or butter over high heat while stirring or tossing frequently. It's ideal for vegetables, proteins, and delicate ingredients.

- Use a heavy skillet or sauté pan and get it ripping hot before adding oil
- Don't overcrowd the pan. Cook in small batches if needed
- Toss and flip ingredients regularly to promote even browning
- Consider finishing with an aromatic like garlic, herbs, or lemon zest

Roasting

Roasting uses dry, indirect heat in the oven to cook foods resulting in a delicious concentrated flavor and crispy, browned exterior.

- Preheat the oven to at least 400°F
- Toss veggies/proteins in oil, salt and pepper before roasting
- Use a rimmed baking sheet or shallow pan for even air circulation

- Flip or toss items halfway through roasting time

Steaming

One of the healthiest cooking methods is steaming. Steaming uses hot vapor to gently cook ingredients while preserving the nutrients, color, and fresh flavors.

- Use a steamer basket set over a pot, rimmed pan or Instant Pot insert
- Layer dense vegetables like potatoes on bottom
- Add just enough water to create steam without boiling dry
- Replenish water level as needed during steaming

No matter which method you use, the key is to pay attention throughout the cooking process rather than walking away. Notice the changes in aroma, texture, and appearance. This mindfulness results in mastering techniques and creating perfectly cooked dishes.

Here's a couple of additional cooking techniques using other cooking appliances that you may have heard of. For both of these appliances, take time to understand manufacturer instructions to prevent safety issues or food mishaps. Allow the devices to bring ease to your cooking while staying present throughout. Observe, learn, adjust, and enjoy!

Air Frying

Air fryers have become popular for creating crispy "fried" foods using just a small amount of oil and convection heat. Benefits include faster cook times and healthier results.

- Preheat the air fryer to ensure ideal crispy texture
- Arrange foods in a single layer with space between pieces
- Use just a light mist of oil to coat the food

- Shake or toss the basket every 5 minutes for even browning
- Check frequently until you learn ideal cook times

Notice the smells wafting out as foods transform into a crispy delight. The air fryer allows you to satisfy cravings in a more nutritious way.

Instant Pot

This electric pressure cooker is a powerhouse for making meals fast while retaining nutrients. From stews to grains to yogurt, the possibilities are endless.

- Read instructions carefully as pressurized cooking is precise
- Use just enough liquid to create steam
- Secure lid properly and ensure vent is sealed
- Allow natural or quick pressure release based on the recipe
- Adjust cook times as needed depending on quantities

Appreciate the convenience while honoring the process. The steam being released will be very hot. Do not attempt to remove the lid until all steam has been released.

Building a Spice Pantry

Not a master chef? No problem. Start simple by properly seasoning foods and letting high-quality ingredients shine. With time, your skills and confidence in the kitchen will grow.

Spices are powerhouse ingredients that can transform a basic dish into an explosion of delicious flavors and aromas. But beyond just their taste benefits, spices also pack a nutritional punch of antioxidants, anti-inflammatory compounds, and other health-promoting qualities.

Buy spices from reputable sources and inspect for vibrant colors and potent aromas. Replace bottles yearly as spices lose potency over time. Things to know:

- Warm spices - cinnamon, nutmeg, cloves, and allspice
- Earthy/smoky spices - cumin, coriander, and smoked paprika
- Robust spices - black pepper, cayenne, and chili powder
- Fresh and dried green herbs - parsley, cilantro, dill, oregano, thyme, rosemary, and sage

How to Use Spices Mindfully

- Combine complementary spices like chili and garlic, or cinnamon and cardamom
- Bloom spices in oil or butter to unlock their essential oils and aromas
- Add hearty spices earlier in cooking for maximum flavor infusion
- Use more delicate spices like saffron just before serving
- Start with smaller amounts and adjust to your taste preferences

Spice Benefits

Different spices offer unique health-promoting properties:

- Turmeric contains curcumin to fight inflammation
- Ginger aids digestion and has anti-nausea effects
- Cinnamon can help regulate blood sugar levels
- Chili peppers provide metabolism-boosting capsaicin

Expand your spice horizons by experimenting with global blends like curry powder, garam masala, and Chinese five spice. Let them awaken your senses. Fortify your dishes with antioxidants and disease-fighting compounds. Using a vibrant array of spices allows you to reduce reliance on salt, sugar, and unhealthy fats for flavor. Embrace spices as a path towards nutritious, mindfully seasoned meals.

Mindful Eating

As you cook, breathe in the aroma of herbs and spices. Let the rhythmic actions of chopping, stirring, and plating become a form of meditation. Cooking provides a lens into giving yourself the gift of nourishing sustenance.

When plating your meal, arrange it in a visually appealing way that whets your appetite. Notice the colors, shapes, and textures coming together. Use smaller plates/bowls to control portions and make meals look abundant. Then add a garnish like fresh herbs, edible flowers, or lemon wedges. This sets an intention toward mindful appreciation from your first bite.

Finally, sit down at a table without distractions to experience your meal. Before diving in pause to give thanks for the meal's journey to your plate. Chew slowly and deliberately to tune into the interplay of flavors and sensations. Each bite holds a chance to savor the miracle of Life energy transferring into your body. Notice when you start to feel full and stop eating at 80% satisfied. Mindful eating doesn't require being perfect. Just be present and appreciate what you are eating more fully. Over time, these intentional practices will reconnect you to eating as a sacred act of nourishment.

23

Exercise Made Easy

I think it's beneficial to break exercise into two categories: functional and planned workouts. Functional exercise is about finding ways to move more throughout the day by making small adjustments to how you do everyday tasks.

For instance, turn household chores into mini-workouts by adding extra effort such as doing lunges while vacuuming. If you take public transportation, consider getting off one stop early and walking the rest of the way. If you drive, try parking farther away from your destination to add a few more steps to your day.

These movements may not seem like much on their own, but they add up over time, contributing to your overall fitness and well-being.

Examples of Functional Exercise

- Household chores
- Taking the stairs
- Chasing children at the park
- Gardening
- Grocery and clothes shopping
- Simply running errands

To maximize the benefits of functional exercise, try engaging your core. Whether you're walking, standing in line, or reaching for something on a shelf, consciously engage your core muscles. This not only strengthens your abs but also improves posture and stability.

Approach everyday activities with intention. For instance, when you walk, do so briskly and with purpose. Imagine each step is part of your workout and you'll naturally increase your pace and energy. Wear the proper footwear even if you need to carry your heels with you in a tote bag.

When standing in line stretch your arms, legs, and back. These small stretches keep your muscles limber and prevent stiffness. How about doing some squats before sitting down in a chair?

Challenge yourself to find creative ways to move more each day. I'm sure you can think of lots more little things like this to seamlessly get some additional movement into your day. What are some other ways you can think of to kick it up a notch?

Planned Workouts

Planned workouts are where you can really amp it up. Depending on where your fitness level is right now, this will look different for each person. The goal is a well-balanced and enjoyable exercise to where you break a sweat. Start by finding your comfort zone. Then challenge yourself a little at a time with more vigor. Don't just go through the motions.

Think about endurance and strength. Planned workouts should include a good balance of cardio and strength training.

Variety Is Key. Mix up your cardio routine to keep it interesting and to work different muscle groups. You might alternate between walking, running, cycling, and swimming. If you're indoors, try activities like dancing, using a rowing machine, or following an aerobic workout video.

Incorporate interval training into your cardio sessions by alternating between periods of high-intensity exercise and lower-intensity recovery. This approach not only increases calorie burn but also boosts your fitness level more quickly.

To ensure you're working at the right intensity, consider using a heart rate monitor. Aim to exercise within your target heart rate zone to maximize cardiovascular benefits while avoiding overexertion.

Aim for getting into a sweat. Getting into a sweat through physical exercise is important for several reasons. Training at an intensity that induces sweating builds your stamina over time. You'll gradually be able to exercise harder and longer without fatigue as your body becomes more conditioned.

The bottom line is that working up a sweat through sustained, vigorous movement is a sign that you are exerting yourself enough to trigger the full-body benefits of exercise.

Cardiovascular Health

When you exert yourself to the point of sweating, it means you are raising your heart rate and breathing rate. This strengthens your cardiovascular system over time by conditioning your heart muscle and improving blood flow and oxygen delivery throughout your body.

Calorie Burning

Breaking a sweat generally indicates you are working out at a higher intensity level. The more intense the workout, the more calories you'll burn. This aids in weight management and can boost your metabolism even after the workout is over.

Detoxification

Sweat is one of your body's methods for expelling waste products and toxins. When you sweat, it helps remove substances like BPA, phthalates, and even heavy metals and environmental pollutants that can accumulate in tissues.

Skin Health

The act of sweating helps flush bacteria out of sweat ducts and pores. It also helps regulate body temperature to prevent overheating. The salt in sweat even has natural antimicrobial properties.

Stress Relief

Exercise that works up a sweat causes your body to release endorphins. These chemical compounds elevate mood and reduce stress and tension. Physical activity can improve mental health and sleep quality.

Strength Training

Strength, weight, or as some may refer to as resistance training is an important component of overall physical fitness and holistic wellness. For a comprehensive routine, include multi-joint exercises like squats, lunges, pushes, pulls, and core work that engage major muscle groups. Gradually increase weight, reps, and intensity for sustainable progressive overload. Proper form is crucial to avoid injury and achieve optimal muscle-building results. Be mindful of balancing your activities with both enjoyment and progression.

Strength training breaks down muscle fibers, which then rebuild stronger. Make sure to allow sufficient recovery time between sessions for the same muscle group, and include activities like stretching, foam rolling, or light yoga to aid in recovery. Flexibility and mobility are often overlooked but are vital components of a well-rounded fitness routine. Improved flexibility helps prevent injury, reduces muscle tension, and enhances overall movement efficiency. Here are some key benefits of incorporating weight training:

Increased Muscle Mass and Strength

By putting resistance on your musculoskeletal system, weight training causes micro-tears in muscle fibers. As these muscle fibers repair, the muscles become stronger and more developed over time. This builds lean muscle mass which supports a faster resting metabolism.

Better Bone Density

The pulling and pushing forces created by weight training put healthy stress on bones. This stimulates them to increase mineral density and become stronger and more fracture-resistant, which is especially important as we age.

Improved Mobility and Balance

Lifting weights requires your muscles to coordinate and stabilize joints through complex movement patterns. This enhances flexibility, range of motion, posture, and overall functional strength and balance.

More Calorie Burn

Muscle is metabolically more active than fat, so having more lean mass means you burn more calories at rest. Weight training also torches a lot of calories during and after the workout.

Disease Prevention

Studies link higher muscle mass with reduced risks of chronic conditions like heart disease, diabetes, osteoporosis, and certain cancers. Strength training improves insulin sensitivity, blood pressure, cholesterol levels, and more.

Mental Health Benefits

The focus and mind-body connection required during weight workouts can be meditative. Exercise also increases endorphins, dopamine, and growth factors that elevate mood and cognition.

*"Self-care is giving the world
the best of you,
instead of what's left of you."
– Katie Reed*

24

Personal Hygiene and Radiant Skin

In your journey of personal growth and transformation, one of the most profound acts of love is the commitment to nurture your personal hygiene care needs. For too long, many of us have lived at the mercy of unrelenting demands, self-criticism, and the unspoken belief that prioritizing our needs is an indulgence rather than a necessity.

Just like how a wildflower cannot bloom if it's neglected and deprived of sunlight and nourishment, you also need intentional and consistent self-care and nourishment to thrive. You are a valuable individual with unique gifts, limitless potential, and deep worth. Taking care of your overall well-being with care and commitment is not selfish. Rather, it's a way to honor and appreciate the miracle of your existence.

Creating a nurturing self-care plan is an act of embracing deep self-love and compassion. It involves restructuring your daily, weekly, and monthly routine and shaping a life filled with nourishing habits that treat your mind, body, and spirit as precious priorities. It's a steadfast commitment to replenish your energy, passion, and joy through personalized practices that cater to your personal care giving needs.

Self-care is not a luxury, it's the nourishing foundation that allows you to thrive and grow into your fullest potential.

The Power of Deep Breathing

Few things are as under-utilized as conscious deep breathing. The ancient practice of using full, nourishing breaths has been shown to have profound benefits for both body and mind. From reducing stress and anxiety to improving focus and sleeping better at night, deep breathing exercises are a simple way to cultivate a greater sense of health and well-being.

On a physiological level, deep breathing helps maximize the flow of oxygen to cells while allowing fuller expulsion of carbon dioxide waste from your body. This exchange of gases supports the optimal functioning of all your body's systems. Full inhalations cause the diaphragm to move downward, massaging and stimulating your organs. This aids digestion, circulation, and detoxification. Meanwhile, the exhalations allow your abdominal muscles to relax, releasing tension and stress.

Psychologically, deep breathing helps calm your mind by activating the parasympathetic nervous system which is your "rest and digest" mode that counteracts your fight-or-flight stress response. As your mental focus is placed on the rhythm of each inhale and exhale, your mind becomes absorbed in the present moment rather than dwelling on the past or worrying about the future. This mindful awareness induces a natural sense of tranquility and centeredness.

Deep Breathing Exercise

To practice deep breathing, find a comfortable seated position with a straight spine. Place one hand on your abdomen to feel the rise and fall. Inhale slowly through your nose, consciously expanding your belly with your diaphragm. Pause briefly, then exhale fully through gently pursed lips, allowing your abdomen to deflate completely. Visualize any tension leaving your body with each exhalation.

Start with cycles that include 4 counts of inhaling and 6 counts of exhaling. Breathe into your lower belly, and allow your abdomen to expand fully before your chest rises. Over time, work up to 6-8 breaths per minute for maximum stress relief and healing benefits.

Whether first thing in the morning, during work breaks, or before bedtime, spending just 5-10 minutes to focus on this ancient breathing practice provides a powerful self-care ritual. Deep breathing is free, convenient, and remarkably effective for harmonizing your body, calming your mind, and enabling you to truly relax into the present moment of your life.

Achieving a Clear, Radiant Complexion

Our skin is the body's largest organ. It serves as a protective barrier while also reflecting our inner health and wellness. Investing time into a consistent skincare routine is crucial not just for a glowing appearance, but for maintaining overall skin health and vitality. Here are the key practices to incorporate:

Gentle Cleansing

Facial skin is thinner and more delicate than skin on the body, with more active oil glands but less hydrating oils. Our face also has a higher density of visible pores. Pores are tiny openings in the skin that allow sweat and oils to be released. Keeping pores clear helps prevent acne breakouts and allows skin to breathe properly. Washing your face daily with a mild, non-drying cleanser suited to your skin type is essential for removing dirt, oil, makeup, and other pore-clogging impurities.

For your body, you should also avoid harsh soaps that can strip away your skin's protective oils. Short warm daily showers using a creamy, fragrance-free body wash helps to cleanse and remove dirt, bacteria, and excess oil from pores without excessive dryness.

Aside from that, choose a specific day once a week or so when you have time for a bath. Create a welcoming bathing space by clearing away clutter and adding soft lighting and appealing fragrances from natural soaps, bath salts, or essential oils. As you bathe, tune into the sensation of warm water caressing your skin. Breathe deeply. Use a soft loofah, cloth, or just your hands to slowly massage areas that feel tense or sore. This is your time to simply be present with yourself.

Ample Moisture

Replenishing moisture daily is vital for keeping your skin soft, and supple. It also helps prevent premature wrinkles. Look for face and body moisturizers that contain hydrating ingredients like hyaluronic acid, glycerin, ceramides, or antioxidants. Apply moisturizer to slightly damp skin to lock in hydration. Quality formulas won't clog pores.

Weekly Exfoliation

Removing built-up dead skin cells through gentle exfoliation 1-2 times per week leaves a smoother, brighter complexion. Use a face scrub with microbeads or a soft washcloth and avoid overly abrasive products. Dry brushing with a soft natural bristle brush before showering also improves circulation and removes dead skin cells. I've included instructions for dry brushing below this skincare section.

Balanced Diet

What you eat has a major influence on your skin's health and radiance. A diet rich in vitamin C, vitamin E, and other plant antioxidants from colorful fruits and veggies help neutralize free radicals that damage skin cells and deplete collagen. This keeps skin firm and vibrant. Lean proteins, healthy fats from foods like avocados and fatty fish improve skin's moisture levels and flexibility. Zinc and B-vitamin sources like eggs, seeds, lentils, and nutritional yeast promote cellular renewal, collagen production, and overall skin rejuvenation for an even skin tone and a radiant complexion.

Diets high in processed foods, unhealthy fats, and refined carbs can lead to inflammation, impaired collagen, oiliness, and breakouts.

Hydration

Stay hydrated by drinking plenty of water daily to aid detoxification and improve overall circulation and skin vitality. Adequate hydration helps flush toxins from the body for a clear complexion. Aim for about 8 cups of water a day.

Sun Protection

Applying a broad-spectrum sunscreen with SPF 30 or higher to any exposed skin daily (and reapplying every two hours outdoors) provides crucial protection against damaging UV rays, age spots, premature aging, and skin cancer risk. Seek shade during peak sun hours when possible.

Adequate Sleep

Tiredness reduces circulation to your face and eyes. When you don't get enough quality sleep the tiny capillaries under your eyes dilate and leak fluids. This makes the under-eye area appear darkened and puffy as blood pools there. Poor circulation also means fluids aren't drained away efficiently, allowing them to accumulate under the eyes.

Treat Your Body

In addition to your daily skincare routine, indulging in self-care practices like professional massages every 4-6 weeks supports lymphatic drainage, improves circulation, and reduces stressed tight facial muscles. *Dry brushing and at-home self-massage using *facial massage tools can be incorporated as well. I've included both the instructions for dry brushing and some suggestions for facial massage tools below this skincare section.

Shaving Right

For smooth hair-free skin, shave after bathing/showering when hair is softened. Replace razors frequently and always use shaving cream/

gel and warm water to prevent irritation and nicks. Men should apply a nutrient-rich aftershave lotion without alcohol. Exfoliating beforehand removes dead skin for a closer shave.

Anti-Aging Treatments

Middle-aged women may benefit from specialized anti-aging treatments like retinol creams, peptide serums or masks to minimize wrinkles, age spots and loss of firmness. Getting monthly facials tailored to your skin's needs or investing in at-home facial massage tools can also reveal a more youthful, luminous glow.

By caring for your skin inside and out through cleansing, moisture replenishment, exfoliation, diet, hydration, sun protection, dry brushing, and massage treatments, you'll not only look radiant but you will also strengthen your skin's resilience for overall beauty and confidence at every age.

The Ancient Practice of Dry Skin Brushing

While it may sound like an unusual ritual, dry brushing your skin has been used for centuries in many cultures as a way to detoxify the body and rejuvenate the complexion. This simple yet powerful practice involves brushing the entire body with a dry natural bristle brush to exfoliate and stimulate different organ systems.

The Benefits of Dry Brushing

By gently removing dull, dead skin cells, dry brushing allows better detoxification through your skin's surface. It also increases circulation and lymph flow to help remove metabolic wastes and toxins that can accumulate in your body over time. This detox process enhances your skin's radiance and provides a healthy glow.

In addition to aiding elimination, dry brushing helps "unstick" and dislodge hardened fats, acids, and toxins that can become trapped in fat cells and soft tissues. It quite literally brushes away this buildup, reducing unsightly cellulite and promoting smoother skin texture.

As a form of gentle exfoliation, dry brushing improves the absorption of skincare products by removing the barrier that dead skin can create. It also stimulates collagen production for firmer, more youthful skin over time.

The Proper Technique

For maximum benefits, dry brushing should ideally be done daily before showering or bathing. Use a long-handled, natural bristle brush with a removable head to easily reach all areas. The bristles should be stiff but not overly rough.

Start at your feet. Use light brush strokes in an upward motion to guide lymph flow toward your heart. Work up your legs, across your abdomen, down your arms, back and shoulders. Give extra attention to areas prone to cellulite like the hips and thighs. Avoid any broken or irritated skin.

Brush for just 2-5 minutes using moderate pressure, just enough to stimulate circulation but not enough to cause abrasions. Afterward, take a warm shower or bath to gently cleanse your now exfoliated skin.

Finish with an all-over body oil or moisturizer serum to nourish and hydrate. Layering on a body oil or cream after dry brushing and cleansing will also help the moisturizer penetrate more deeply for intense softening.

Facial Massage

Facial massage is both an invigorating and soothing practice that enhances circulation, promotes lymphatic drainage, and gives your skin a healthy glow. To begin, start with a clean face and hands. Apply a small amount of facial oil or your favorite moisturizer to your face to provide a smooth glide for your fingers. Using gentle, upward strokes, begin by massaging your forehead with your fingertips moving from the center out towards your temples. Then, on your cheeks use circular motions to lift and sculpt the area from your nose to your ears. Next, focus on your jawline and chin. Use your thumbs to apply gentle pressure in an upward motion following the contours of your jaw. Around your eye, gently use your ring fingers to lightly tap around your eyes, starting from the inner corner and moving outward. Finish by massaging your neck with upward strokes to encourage circulation and help lift the skin.

Regular facial massage can relax facial muscles, reduce puffiness, and leave your skin looking refreshed and rejuvenated. Using any of the following facial massage tools 2-3 times per week along with a facial massage cream or serum can take your skincare game to the next level for a radiant, contoured, and glowing complexion.

Gua Sha Tool

This flat, curved jade or rose quartz stone massage tool is used with gentle scraping motions to improve circulation, drain lymph fluid, and relieve tension. Using a gua sha tool regularly can help depuff, sculpt, and give you a natural lift.

Jade Roller

A jade roller has a small roller ball at one end and a larger one at the other. Rolling the cool jade stone over your face and neck helps de-puff, calm inflammation, and boost blood flow while giving you a relaxing face massage.

Face Massage Wands

These handheld wands have differently shaped stone or metallic tips to target specific areas like under-eyes, laugh lines, jaw tension, etc. The different contours allow you to really work into hard-to-reach spots.

Microneedling Derma Roller

While not a massage tool per se, derma rollers covered in tiny needles can be rolled over the face to create micro-injuries that trigger collagen production for firmer, more youthful skin. Use it before applying serums for deeper absorption.

The Importance of Good Oral Hygiene

Oral hygiene is an often overlooked but crucial component of personal care that contributes significantly to overall health and well-being. Just as caring for your skin requires a daily routine to maintain its vibrancy and youthfulness, maintaining good oral hygiene is essential for preserving not only your smile but also your general health. The mouth serves as a gateway to the body, and neglecting it can lead to a host of issues that extend far beyond cavities and gum disease.

A consistent oral hygiene routine begins with brushing your teeth at least twice a day, ideally after meals, to remove plaque and food particles that can contribute to tooth decay and gum disease. It's equally important to replace your toothbrush every three to four months, or sooner if the bristles become frayed, as worn-out bristles can be less effective at cleaning your teeth.

Flossing daily is another critical aspect of oral hygiene. While brushing cleans the surface of your teeth, flossing removes food particles and plaque from between the teeth and under the gumline, areas where a toothbrush can't reach. Neglecting to floss can lead to the buildup of plaque, which can harden into tartar. Tartar buildup can lead to gum disease which has been linked to systemic conditions like heart disease and diabetes.

By prioritizing the care of your teeth and gums, you're investing in your long-term well-being, ensuring that your body is as healthy on the inside as it appears on the outside.

*"You yourself, as much as anybody
in the entire universe,
deserve your love and affection."
− Buddha*

25

Designing a Nurturing Self-Care Plan

Making self-love and self-care a priority allows you to show up as your best self in all areas of life. Designing an intentional, nurturing self-care plan can help ensure you are carving out vital time for replenishing your mind, body, and spirit.

1. Start by Checking In

Begin by doing an honest self-assessment. In what areas do you feel depleted or stressed currently? What activities or practices truly light you up and help you feel recharged? Identify your unique needs and what resonates most with your personal definition of self-love.

2. Make a List

Based on your reflections, compile a list of potential self-care activities to incorporate across different dimensions of wellness such as physical, emotional, spiritual, social, and intellectual.

Sample List:
- Exercise/movement practices
- Preparing nourishing meals
- Journaling/reading inspirational books
- Spending time in nature
- Creative pursuits/hobbies
- Unplugging from technology
- Quality social connection
- Continuing education
- Restful sleep habits

3. Schedule It

With your list as inspiration, get out your calendar and start scheduling self-care appointments with yourself for the week ahead. Ideally, spread these different activities throughout. Prioritize your availability and block off these important time slots before anything else gets booked.

4. Start Small

Be realistic about how much you can commit to currently. It's better to start with 10-15 minutes per day to build a habit, rather than overwhelming yourself with unrealistic expectations that lead to self-judgement.

5. Create Routines and Rituals

As you discover which self-care activities are most enjoyable and beneficial you can build routines and rituals around them to ingrain new patterns. For example, you might want to wake up earlier for journaling and meditation, plan a regular day and time for an evening bath ritual, and create a dedicated veggie prep workstation in your kitchen, equipped with storage containers that make it easy to prepare and store nutritious vegetables. This setup will help ensure you always have healthy, ready-to-use veggies on hand for your meals.

6. Embrace Spirituality

Spirituality is a deeply personal journey. It is an exploration of the soul, an inquiry into the meaning and purpose of life that encourages self-reflection, inner growth, and a deeper understanding of the world around us. At its core, spirituality is about cultivating a connection with the divine, the universe, or whatever you believe. This connection often manifests as a sense of peace, fulfillment, and clarity that guides you toward living a life that aligns with your true essence.

Embracing spirituality often involves practices such as meditation, prayer, mindfulness, or spending time in nature serving as a conduit to deeper awareness and connection. These practices can help quiet the mind, allowing you to tune into an inner voice and gain insight into your purpose and passions. Spirituality also fosters a sense of interconnectedness with others and the world, nurturing compassion, empathy, and a desire to contribute positively to the greater good. Ultimately, spirituality is about seeking harmony within yourself and with the universe, finding meaning in life's experiences, and living in alignment with your highest values and truths.

7. Get Support

Share your intentions with loved ones who can support your efforts and hold you accountable. Politely set boundaries where needed to honor your self-nurturing time. You can also join communities focused on self-love and personal growth.

Use the following checklist as a general guide to help you design a daily, weekly, and monthly self-care plan. Customize your practices to align with your preferences and needs. Prioritize simplicity and efficiency so that it feels natural and easy to follow. The key is to design a balanced plan that integrates a variety of practices across multiple areas to nurture yourself holistically. Treat this as an ongoing process of self-discovery as your needs and desires evolve over time. With consistency you can truly thrive from the inside out.

Mind-Body-Spirt Self-Care Checklist

Physical Self-Care:
☐ Regular exercise that aligns with your fitness goals and preferences.
☐ Balanced and nutritious diet to nourish your body.
☐ Sufficient and quality sleep for optimal rest and recovery.
☐ Hydration to ensure you're drinking an adequate amount of water.

Emotional and Mental Well-Being:
☐ Daily mindfulness or meditation practice for stress reduction.
☐ Journaling to express and reflect on your thoughts and emotions.
☐ Time for hobbies and activities that bring you joy and relaxation.
☐ Establish healthy boundaries to protect your emotional well-being.

Social Connections:
☐ Regular quality time with friends and loved ones.
☐ Engage in activities that foster social connections.
☐ Communicate openly and honestly in your relationships.
☐ Seek support when needed and nurture positive connections.

Personal Development:
☐ Set and work towards personal and professional goals.
☐ Continuous learning and skill development.

☐ Reading or consuming content that inspires and motivates you.
☐ Reflection on your values and life purpose.

Rest and Relaxation:

☐ Scheduled downtime for rest and relaxation.
☐ Regular breaks during work or daily tasks.
☐ Incorporate activities that promote relaxation at home and in nature.
☐ Practice deep breathing or other relaxation techniques.

Self-Compassion and Positive Affirmations:

☐ Positive self-talk and affirmations.
☐ Cultivate self-compassion in moments of challenge.
☐ Forgive yourself for mistakes and imperfections.
☐ Celebrate achievements, no matter how small.

Skincare and Grooming:

☐ Establish a skincare routine that suits your skin type.
☐ Grooming activities that make you feel good about your appearance.
☐ Self-care practices like massages or spa treatments.

Digital Detox:

☐ Set boundaries on screen time.
☐ Schedule regular breaks from social media.
☐ Disconnect from devices before bedtime.

Regular Self-Reflection:

☐ Periodically review and adjust your self-love and care routine.
☐ Assess what's working well and what might need improvement.
☐ Stay attuned to changes in your needs and priorities.

"Self-care is how you take your power back."
— Lalah Delia

26

Path to Purpose Passion, Joy, and Fulfillment

What does it mean to live a truly fulfilling life? For many, it begins with discovering your purpose. It's that driving force that motivates you and gives your life deeper meaning. When you uncover your unique purpose and align it with your passions, an incredible sense of joy can emerge.

Discovering Your Life's Purpose

Your life purpose is the compass that guides you. It represents your core values and the positive impact you want to make on the world around you. Reflecting on the times you have felt most alive and inspired can provide clues to your purpose. What activities energize you? What causes or beliefs stir you at your deepest level? Your purpose likely lies at the intersection of the things you care most deeply about and your unique gifts and talents.

Pursuing Your Passions

Passion encompasses the interests, hobbies, career paths and creative pursuits that you find deeply engaging and fulfilling. When you regularly participate in activities you are passionate about, time seems to slow as you become fully immersed in the experience. Your passions shouldn't feel like work. They should be the areas of life where you find joy, flow and intrinsic motivation.

Cultivating Sustained Joy

While fleeting pleasures provide momentary happiness, the path to sustained, soul-level joy is walking in alignment with your purpose and passions. When you spend your days doing work that matters to you and allowing your creative spirit to be expressed, you experience profound fulfillment. Embracing gratitude, living with authenticity, and serving others in a way that leverages your talents are key to maintaining this state of joy.

Crafting Your Fulfilling Life

Discovering and honoring your life's purpose takes courage, self-reflection and commitment. It means saying no to the inauthentic demands of daily life to say yes to living with intention and meaning. As you identify and nourish your core passions and connect them to how you want to contribute to the world, a rich and fulfilling life emerges. With purpose as your guide and passion as your fuel, unbridled joy becomes possible.

However, our sense of purpose is not a static, unchanging force. It is an ever-evolving insight that takes new shape through the pivotal milestones we encounter. The purpose that stirs you as an ambitious career starter may grace you with an entirely different focus once you become a parent. Similarly, redefining your purpose is often essential when you've reached the glory of the empty nest stage or embark on your life's wise elder years. Let's explore how our life's purpose can profoundly shift across these transformative stages:

Purpose in Your Career

For many, a career acts as the main driver of purpose during your working years. Feeling that your work matters and contributes something positive can inspire even routine tasks with greater meaning. Your career purpose may be to excel in your field, serve clients well, create innovative solutions, or make a difference through the work itself. As you progress in your career, that sense of purpose may evolve from paying dues early on to striving for impact by providing mentorship.

The Purpose of Parenting

Raising children brings an entirely new dimension of purpose for many people. The role of a parent gives you the profound opportunity to nurture young lives, shape the next generation, and leave a legacy through your values and guidance. Your parenting purpose may center on cultivating caring citizens of the world or empowering your children to pursue their passions and potential. As their needs change from infancy to adolescence, so too may your core purpose as a parent.

Purpose in the Empty Nest

After celebrating the accomplishments of launching children into the world, many empty nesters find themselves re-evaluating their purpose during this new phase of life. You may be drawn to finally pursue deferred dreams, achieve daring goals, or consider an encore career aligned with your deepest beliefs. Alternatively, your purpose may involve embracing the freedom of this stage through traveling, investing in treasured relationships, and adopting a giving spirit.

Golden Years' Purpose

In later years, your sense of purpose may likely be about sharing your lifetime of accumulated wisdom. You may feel called to invest in causes that create a better world or simply to savor life's daily joys more thoughtfully. Leaving an impactful legacy through philanthropy, volunteerism, or insights gained over many years can become a driving purpose.

Your lived experience has granted you profound insights. Through mentorship or developing educational programs, you can share your life's lessons for others to benefit from. Using the resources and influence you can curate you might like to become involved in initiatives, and environmental projects, or contribute to social impact organizations as avenues for making your mark in the world.

In later years, you have the opportunity to solidify the ideals and causes that deeply resonate with you. Whether through sharing wisdom or simply setting a lasting example through your actions, your purpose in later life is connected to the lasting impact you leave behind. It can be as simple as telling a story to your grandchild that they remember and then tell to their grandchildren. The lives you touch every day become the best legacy of all. Your legacy serves as a testament to your values, and it's entrusted to those who will continue to carry the torch forward in the years ahead

The Kindling of Passion

Passion often begins with a tiny spark as a pursuit that captivates your interest and imagination in a way that is both deeply felt and profound. For some, those first glimmers of passion can arrive during childhood. It could be the young child captivated by their firefighter uncle, igniting dreams of one day being a hero who rescues others from danger. Alternatively, it could be the 8-year-old losing themselves for hours writing elaborate tales, foreshadowing a passion for storytelling. An early passion may be born from experiences, interests, or influential figures that unlocked an innate sense of curiosity, purpose, or flow state within us from a tender age.

As these childhood passions take root, they begin to consume more of our thoughts, time, and energy. We may actively seek out knowledge, training, and opportunities related to this newfound interest. Passion distinguishes itself from a mere hobby through its intensity and the meaning it provides.

For others, passion strikes like a bolt of lightning during adolescence or adulthood. It could be the first time you explore a creative outlet like painting, sewing, or writing and lose complete track of time. Your fire can ignite when you first see someone or something that perks your interest or when you volunteer for a cause that stirs your soul. Whenever that spark ultimately arrives, it sets your very soul ablaze in a way that mere casual interests cannot.

The Evolution of Passion

What begins as a singular passion can often evolve into a multitude of interconnected passions over time. Sometimes it can veer off in unexpected directions. The young firefighter enthusiast may discover a passion for community service, sustainable urban planning, or environmental activism rather than the firefighting role itself. The enthusiastic writer may gravitate towards journalism, marketing, or podcasting as their passions evolve to intersect with new skills and life callings.

The more you invest yourself fully into a passion, the more it flourishes into a constantly expanding field of exploration and expression. A writer's passion for storytelling may spark or awaken adjacent passions for human psychology or effective public speaking. A volunteer's passion for charity may give rise to passions for community building, nonprofit management, or policy reform.

Passions also have a profound way of evolving alongside your personal growth and transformations. The interests and desires that once delighted you as hobbies or passion projects in your youth ultimately give way to elevated passions more reflective of your matured values and perspectives. Hobbies certainly can fall by the wayside. But the ones where you have an authentic drive and passion for, demand an increasing sense of purpose and impact. Passions that survive this refining process become core pieces of your evolving identity over time.

At times, your passions may even seem to uproot themselves entirely from the course you had charted, blossoming into new hybrid callings you could not have foreseen. Similar to how intense heat and pressure transform rock into metamorphic rock, life experiences can combine and reshape your passions into something entirely new. What was once a passion for teaching may transform into a passion for education reform. A passion for scientific discovery may divert into a passion for bioethics. Such evolutions shouldn't be seen as abandoning your passions. They should be seen as allowing them to become more transcendent.

Throughout your life, your truest passions persevere and mature as you gain wisdom, face pivotal moments, and connect more soulfully with your purpose. They continue to provide deep sources of joy, endless curiosity, and meaningful expression as long as you honor and nurture them. Passion isn't just about fleeting interests; it's a constantly evolving expression of your innermost drive.

The Radiance of Joy

While passion drives your interests with eager energy and pursuit, joy is the radiant light that comes from the depths of your being when you are living fully aligned with your truth. Joy does not come from temporary pleasures or superficial amusements. Rather, it blossoms from a state of harmony and alignment with your mind, body, and spirit's core purpose and deepest passions.

For some, joy arises from creative expression such as artfully bringing your inner vision to life through painting, music, or a finely crafted story. For others, joy flows from awe-inspiring moments, like the spine-tingling witnessing of a heartfelt performance on stage or connecting with nature's majestic beauty. Wherever you discover your deepest sources of happiness and engagement, is where your soul lights up with joy.

Joy acts as a soothing balm, nurturing and replenishing you even during life's toughest challenges and stresses. Joy serves as a reminder of the worthiness of your passions and is a revitalizing pleasure that infuses purpose into your existence.

While passion is your driving force, joy is the experience that makes your pursuits feel profoundly vital and worthwhile. It is what refuels your spirit to stay passionately curious, and engaged with life.

The Culmination of Fulfillment

Ultimately, the brightest joys in your life emerge from a state of fulfillment with a sense that you have manifested your purpose and passions into a life well-lived. It is the integration of all your endeavors, challenges, accomplishments, and innermost drive. It's the crescendo of realizing your aspirations while navigating the lessons of every step that led you there.

Often, fulfillment comes through the creative culmination of your life's distinctive work. It's like the sculptor who adds the final chisel to their work after years of commitment to their craft before stepping back to revel in the totality of their craftsmanship. Or it could be the community activist who realizes the effects of their efforts rippling through improved policies and new opportunities for those they sought to elevate. It could also be the teacher who has the humbling experience of former struggling pupils returning years later as thriving mentors themselves. These glimpses into the timeless impact you impart are what fulfillment's warm embrace feels like.

Fulfillment is the coming together of your highest aspirations, deepest desires, and truest purpose. It's a profound alignment that reveals and embodies your life's purpose with complete satisfaction. Each of us follows a unique path toward these moments of living in harmony with our destiny.

As you are shaped by your experiences, fulfillment ensures that your evolving passions and deepening sense of purpose merge into sources of boundless, untamed joy. It's the ultimate reward for honoring your yearning to live with inspired intensity. By embracing fulfillment, you open yourself to new possibilities and shine brightly as you navigate your next phase of growth.

Conclusion

The keys to unlocking your highest self have been placed firmly in your grasp. Through your courageous inner exploration, you're awakening the dormant gifts that lay within your appreciative spirit, the trust in your instincts, your capacity for deep connection, the wellspring of your life's lessons, and your unshakable self-acceptance. Carry your gifts forth as embodied strengths now.

Take a moment to pause and reflect on how far you've come. The journey hasn't been easy. Facing wounds, challenging limiting beliefs, and embracing profound truths about yourself takes immense courage. Yet, you persisted, driven by a deep desire to unlock your full potential and live a life of purpose, passion, and fulfillment. I firmly believe that the five golden keys open treasure chests of G.I.F.T.S., leading to a life filled with boundless possibilities..

1. The key to the gift of gratitude to awaken you to the beauty that surrounds you each day.

2. Intuitive intentions to aligned you with your authentic self.

3. Nurturing your cherished relationships with family and friends to provide a bedrock of love and support.

4. Embracing your treasured wisdom to give you the knowledge and insights to face life's challenges with grace.

5. And, above all, living in your truth through radical self-love and care as the greatest act of revolution and the dismantling of the chains that once bound you.

As you step forward, let this not be an ending, but a new beginning. A renaissance of your soul. You are the master of your destiny, the author of your life's greatest story. Nurture the dreams that once flickered like distant stars as they now can blaze brilliantly within your grasp. Pursue your passions with unbridled enthusiasm, for your passions will be the compass guiding you to profound happiness, joy, and fulfillment.

You are a phenomenal human being, blessed with infinite gifts yearning to be expressed and shared with a world that desperately needs your light. Wherever the current circumstances of life may be carry this empowering truth:

"You have everything you need to soar into your limitless potential and create a life that is a breathtaking masterpiece."

The possibilities are bound only by the borders of your imagination. So, let your spirit soar into its greatness. Live boldly. Love fiercely. Experience life's majesty. You are the artist and the canvas awaits your brushstrokes of brilliant radiant color. Take this day, and all the ones that follow, and paint the masterpiece of your dreams. I believe in you!

ABOUT THE AUTHOR

Elaine Lombardi is a seasoned travel enthusiast with over seven decades of rich experiences and stories. Through her journey, she's learned the invaluable art of transforming life lessons into wisdom, a gift she believes everyone holds.

With a heart full of passion, Elaine ventured into the realm of online education, striving to empower men and women to rediscover their strengths, share their unique stories, and leave a legacy that resonates.

Elaine Lombardi

Elaine Lombardi is a certified CHHC holistic health coach. With a focus on nutrition, her training at the Institute for Integrative Nutrition included all aspects of well-being as an AADP Board Certified Practitioner by the American Association of Drugless Practitioners.

Aside from her coaching practice, she worked with young adults on the autism spectrum as an Occupational Counselor for the State of California teaching independent living skills, and helping to transition them from living at home to living on their own.

Other certifications she holds include Reiki, EFT, Reflexology, American Red Cross Water Safety Instructor, AFAA Aerobics and Fitness Association of America, and Family and Consumer Studies ECE Early Childhood Education Private Agency Certified Preschool Teacher and Director.

Married for 52 years, she resides in southern California with her husband Michael and rescue dog Frankie. They are the proud parents of four grown children, grandparents of ten grandchildren, and great-grandparents to two great-grandbabies. Elaine enjoys world travel, camping painting and writing.

Her other published books include:

Hurricane Lucy A Caregiver's Guide
Little Lessons, Big Life Journal
Big Teddy Bear: The Colorful New Arrivals

www.ingramcontent.com/pod-product-compliance
Lightning Source LLC
Chambersburg PA
CBHW032031290426
44110CB00012B/760